Bahá'í Parenting Perspectives

Bahá'í Parenting Perspectives

by

Negin and Nima Anvar

George Ronald
Oxford

George Ronald, *Publisher*
Oxford
www.grbooks.com

© Negin and Nima Anvar 2006
All Rights Reserved

A catalogue record for this book is available from the British Library

ISBN 0-85398-502-2

Cover picture: John Barnabas Leith

Printed in Great Britain
by Biddles Ltd, King's Lynn

Contents

Acknowledgements   x
Introduction   xi

1 Helping Your Child Develop a Love for the Faith

When did you first talk to your child about God and how did you introduce Him?   1

Were there ever times when you would allow your children to skip Feast or some other Bahá'í event because of too much schoolwork?   4

Did your child ever not want to attend Feast, children's classes or some other Bahá'í event?   7

What advice would you give to Bahá'í parents living in isolated communities where there are few or no other Bahá'ís?   12

How can we increase Bahá'í influence for our children in an isolated community?   17

How can we define Bahá'í identity for our children?   19

Did you celebrate Christmas? If not, how did you handle not celebrating it?   21

What would you do if your child were approaching the age of maturity and said that she did not wish to be a Bahá'í?   25

2 Teaching Your Child the Principle of Obedience

How did you punish your child? Were privileges withdrawn? Did you give time-outs or did you sometimes prefer to ignore the bad behaviour?   31

BAHÁ'Í PARENTING PERSPECTIVES

What is your opinion on spanking (smacking) – that is, a mild swat on the hand or a swat on the bottom? 35

What did you do about children answering back and always demanding the last word? 38

When and how did you explain to your child some of the laws of the Faith that would apply to them when they reached the age of 15, for example obligatory prayer, fasting and Ḥuqúqu'lláh? 41

3 Teaching Your Child the Principle of Trustworthiness and Integrity

Small children often can't distinguish fact from fiction and are great at making up fantasies or stories when talking to others. By adult standards, this is sometimes considered to be lying. Did you correct your child when this occurred or did you consider this to be a normal part of childhood? 44

What would you do about chronic, persistent lying? 47

What would you do if you found out that your child cheated on a test? 48

From what age did you allow your child to go out without parental supervision? 50

How do you feel about checking on your child from time to time? That is, checking their rooms, diaries, phone calls, etc. 52

Did you allow your children to lock their doors? What if they said, 'It's MY room!' 54

What are your rules on phone calls? 57

4 Helping Your Child Understand the Principles of Chastity and Moderation

At what age did you talk to your child about sex and how did you introduce it? 59

What were your rules on dating? 61

CONTENTS

What were your rules on curfews? 64

How can we encourage our children to have higher moral standards than the society around us without making them feel isolated from classmates? 66

What are your rules on watching TV? 71

Which was more of a concern – sex and sexual images on TV or violence or both? 75

Did you monitor and/or select the music your children listened to? 77

What are your rules on clothes? 79

What would you do if your teenager wanted to get a tattoo? 82

What would you do if your teenager wanted to have his tongue, nose or navel pierced? 84

What is your policy about hairstyles? What if your teenager wanted to dye his hair purple? 87

If you ever suspected that your child had been drinking alcohol, taking drugs or sniffing glue, how would you deal with this? 89

5 School and Peer-Related Issues

Were you selective about the friends that your children made? 91

Once children start school and enter middle childhood (ages six and up), they start to undergo tremendous peer pressure. How can we minimize this? How can we teach our Bahá'í children to be leaders instead of followers? 94

What were your rules on slumber parties and sleep-overs? 96

Your pre-teen daughter comes home from school and is devastated that a friend has shunned her and that she feels excluded from a certain group. How do you help her? 100

Your child gets bullied, picked on or teased. What do you do? 102

BAHÁ'Í PARENTING PERSPECTIVES

If your child came home saying that he needed the 'right' kind of clothes or athletic shoes and was being laughed at for not having them, how would you deal with this? 105

From what age (if at all) did you allow your teenager to attend 'teenage' parties? 108

6 Helping Your Child Understand the Sanctity of the Family

Is it more important to you that you be a parent to your child or a friend/buddy? 111

What did you do when siblings fought? 113

What should be done about sibling rivalry? 115

How did you help your child learn the principle of consultation? 118

How can we teach our kids to be selective and successful when choosing a spouse? 121

What would you do if you felt pressured to give consent for your child's marriage but had doubts? 124

7 Creating a Home Environment Conducive to Material and Spiritual Welfare

Did either one of you stay home to be a full-time parent when the children were young? 127

What are your feelings about daycare? 131

What is your opinion about babysitters? 134

When your children were babies, how would you react to nighttime waking? 138

Did you give your children an allowance? 140

Did you pay your children for chores? 142

What are you looking for in your child's choice of university? Do you have any concerns about college life? 144

CONTENTS

Can you recommend your favourite parenting books?	148
What sort of sacrifices did you have to make in order to parent the way that you saw fit?	151
What, to you, is the most challenging issue(s) facing Bahá'í parents today?	153
What are some of your tips for raising a spiritual and good child, a child with character?	155
If you could parent all over again and knowing what you know now, what would you do differently? How would you advise 'brand new' parents today?	160

8 Meet the Children

How do you think the Bahá'í Faith has affected you throughout your life?	164
How is your life different from the life of your non-Bahá'í friends?	166
What are some of your favourite books and why are they your favourites?	169
Were your career plans affected by the Bahá'í teachings?	172
What will you do differently when you are a parent?	173
What do you appreciate most about your parents?	174
What do you appreciate least about your parents?	176
Looking back, what do you think are the most important things you've learned from your parents?	177
How do you feel about your future?	180

9 Biographies of the Parents	184
Bibliography	191
References	192

Acknowledgements

This book would not exist without the generous help of many parents and their children. These individuals answered questions and offered remarkable insights. We would like to thank each and every one of them for their valuable feedback and assistance. We are greatly indebted to them for their time and effort. We have, however, disguised their names to prevent embarrassment!

Introduction

In a sense, this book has been a work in progress for over seven years. Shortly after the birth of our first child we were overwhelmed with the responsibility of caring for a baby. Like most first-time parents, we had no childcare experience and turned to friends and family for advice. We asked questions about everything. How do you change a diaper? How often do you feed a baby? Will the baby ever sleep through the night? Whenever we couldn't get the answer from our parents or friends, we would rush off to the library to find it in a parenting book.

As time passed and we gained more experience, we began to focus on the spiritual upbringing of our children. We sought advice from other Bahá'í parents who had done a good job bringing up their children. That's when an idea occurred to us. Why couldn't we learn from the 'best practice' of other 'effective' Bahá'í parents? We could make a list of parenting questions and ask parents to answer them. This was the beginning of our parenting book and so we set off on a search for good Bahá'í parents.

Our criteria for inclusion were simple. We either had to personally know the parents and their children or we had to receive recommendations from other Bahá'í parents whom we respected. We also had to be sure that their children had turned out well – that they were Bahá'ís in good standing who were relatively active in the Faith and were leading productive lives.

By the time we had finished our search we had identified 30 couples we considered to be 'effective' Bahá'í parents. We then compiled a list of 50 questions that dealt with practical issues such as tantrums, bullying and dating and asked the parents to respond to them in writing. As you can imagine, there was a wide spectrum of responses with strong opinions on many topics. While we disagreed with some parents, we learned from all of them and now share their lessons with you.

Inside these pages are 300 collective years of parenting experience. Where applicable we have tried to include a variety of parenting approaches so that readers can learn and develop their own style. Unfortunately, some readers may think that the parenting styles presented in the book are the definitive ways of Bahá'í parenting. This is simply not the case. It is important to understand that there is not one best parenting style that fits every family. Every child is different and there will be a myriad of ways to deal with various issues.

Please don't rely on this book to provide *all* the answers. The Bahá'í writings and your own parenting instinct will always remain your best guide. Instead, you can treat this book as a resource to consult during your child's passage from early infancy to adulthood. Pick it up and browse through it from time to time. If your child does not want to attend Feasts, turn to that section. If you are unsure about the amount of TV that your child watches, you can refer to that chapter. This book can be a tool to help you stay ahead of the game and spot problems before they have a chance to hinder your child's spiritual and moral development.

Several thematic issues deserve mention. While we never intended it as such, we realize now that the nature of this book is heavily oriented towards western ideas. That is to say, the majority of the parenting approaches mentioned reflect western influences and ways of thinking. It should also be noted that many issues remained unaddressed by the book. For instance, we did not deal with matters related to step-parenting. This was an oversight on our part. We recognize that many children today live in families with step-parents, and we hope that the parenting approaches mentioned in the book may also broadly apply to them. On a stylistic note, we have chosen to use the generic 'he' in most cases to refer to either girls or boys. We do not intend to be sexist but constant references to he/she are clumsy and awkward.

Finally, no parent is perfect. When compiling this book, we

would often say, 'We know all this and we still keep making mistakes.' We have come to realize that it is the *overall* influence that your child receives that is key, not the occasional slip-ups. The most that any of us can do is to try our hardest for our own children.

1
Helping Your Child Develop a Love for the Faith

When did you first talk to your child about God and how did you introduce Him?

Linda Paulson There was never a formal introduction to God or to the Baháʼí Faith. Our children were born into a family where God, the Central Figures and the teachings of the Baháʼí Faith were always at the forefront. They were born knowing God and we just never let them forget it or move away from Him. We had many tests and difficulties when the children were small. We had lots of prayer sessions – some were 24 hours long. When the children became old enough to participate in these 24-hour prayer sessions, they gladly signed up for a time slot as other family members did.

Angela Brown As you know, Baháʼís are urged by the Master to begin mentioning God to the unborn child while he is still in the womb, praying for him, singing to him and dedicating him to God.

Our youngest son, who just turned 15, is the first of our children who had the complete experience of being conceived by Baháʼí parents. He was born while Hidden Words were sung and special prayers were read. From this time, we sang and said prayers for and with him every morning and evening.

My older daughters began saying prayers morning and evening

from the time I became a Bahá'í. They were then aged five, three and two. They loved their prayer books. They memorized the prayers on each page so that they could open to a prayer, look at the drawing and say the prayer as though they were reading it. Many guests were astounded to see them apparently reading these wonderful prayers from their books, when they were in actuality saying them by heart!

All children are very spiritual when they are small, especially when their mother points out the way God cares for and loves us, what He wants us to do and not to do and how beautiful all of His creation is. Children love stories and we read and told stories to them all at night before bed, then talked about all of their little concerns and what 'Abdu'l-Bahá would have them do. These were times of closeness and reassurance. All of our children have referred to these times with love and yearning. All too soon the children grow up and are no longer interested in having stories read to them and such intimate family chats. But hopefully the seeds of the love of God are planted and will eventually bear fruit, even after the storms of adolescence pass.

The other significant way of helping little ones develop love for God is through the enjoyment of many loving Bahá'ís of all ages and backgrounds and colours. Parents should do everything within their power to be sure that their home is filled with such visitors as often as possible.

Children have a natural affinity with nature and can easily understand the various ways the Creator is hidden and manifest in nature. The beautiful patterns and processes and surprises that teach us about the Beloved of all hearts can be apprehended through nature walks, art, music and science ('. . . until none shall contemplate anything whatsoever but that he shall see God therein').[1]

Bernice McKenzie I became a Bahá'í when I was pregnant with my first daughter. I asked the Bahá'ís around me about praying for and with my baby. Would the baby understand 'the big words'? One of the Bahá'ís told me that a child needs and understands the

DEVELOPING A LOVE FOR THE FAITH

Word of God, just like new fruit on a tree absorbs water. So from that time on, God took a natural part in our lives. I can't really say when I talked to my children about God. It's rather like asking when did I teach them to breathe.

Todd and Debbie McEwen We have said prayers with our children since they were born and talked to them when questions naturally arose. We have never specifically 'introduced' God but always treated Him as being part of our lives.

Fatemeh Pfingston I started singing Bahá'í songs and chanting prayers when I was carrying my children. When they were at the age when they could learn words and phrases, I taught them short words and phrases such as Bahá'u'lláh, 'Abdu'l-Bahá, Alláh-u-Abhá and Huva'lláh. I would show them pictures of 'Abdu'l-Bahá and Bahá'í books and say, 'This is a book by 'Abdu'l-Bahá or Bahá'u'lláh.' I bought them their own prayer books and other Bahá'í books. They were in the room when I said my obligatory prayers and Alláh-u-Abhá 95 times. I took them to Bahá'í meetings and held Bahá'í events at our home from the time they were newborns. To me, God is above my comprehension, so I talked about the Manifestations of God and their teachings. And I encouraged my kids to incorporate positive attributes into their personalities when faced with daily activities, attributes such as honesty, trustworthiness, respect, joy, courage and the completion of tasks.

Irene Dominguez The first thing they learned was to pray together. We have always talked about God, the Almighty. They have attended children's classes from a very young age.

Margerie Gibson We verbally thank God constantly for everything He's given us and for meeting all our needs – our friends, the earth, animals and so on. While cuddling my daughter, I often say 'Thank you, God, for giving me this precious girl to love.' Or I might say to her, 'Aren't we lucky God loves us so much he gave us your wonderful daddy to love us and take care of us?' I weave appreciation and gratitude to God into everything we do. It's as natural as breathing to her, as she's heard about Him all of her life.

Tanya Charles We greeted each of our children with a prayer immediately after birth, said prayers with them each morning and evening from infancy, attended Feasts and Holy Days and, eventually, children's classes. It wasn't a question of introducing God. We've treated belief in God as a given, just as having mom and dad around was a given, no explanation necessary.

We are so fortunate to have a much deeper understanding of God in this Dispensation. I know how much I have appreciated the writings of 'Abdu'l-Bahá when trying to explain difficult concepts. The image of God as a bright sun shining on the mirror of our hearts and of the love of God as the rain falling both on the garden and the garbage dump are simple yet eloquent explanations and are comprehensible to all.

Phoebe Untekar We both talked about God continually from the time our children were born and introduced Him through prayers, songs and stories.

Were there ever times when you would allow your children to skip Feast or some other Bahá'í event because of too much schoolwork?

> ... he cannot but deplore the fact some of the believers are reluctant to observe, as strictly as they should, the Feasts and anniversaries prescribed by the Cause. This attitude, which may be justified in certain exceptional circumstances, is fraught with incalculable dangers and harm to the community, and will, if allowed to persist, seriously endanger its influence and prestige in the public eye. Unity of action, in matters of so vital an importance as the observance of Bahá'í holidays, is essential. It is the responsibility of the N.S.A. to remind and urge the friends to faithfully carry out all such laws and precepts of the Cause, the enforcement of

which does not constitute an open violation of the laws of their country.[2]

Angela Brown As to the priority of Bahá'í events versus academic work, I always think of what the Master said about emphasizing spiritual development over intellectual attainment but when we have both (that is, good character and strong minds) it is light upon light! To me, this means that the 19 Day Feast and Holy Day observances must take priority over academics and sports. But if there is a way to organize things so that both can happen, this is the best way. Yet we are told by the beloved Guardian that we must organize our lives around the Faith, not vice versa. So for Feast nights I have always felt that the Feast should not end abruptly because parents feel their children must go to bed. Rather, I tell my children that there are things more important than sleep. If they become tired, we should give them a cosy, safe place to lie down and be considerate enough not to stay longer than necessary. Often my husband and I would drive two cars, when possible, or cooperate with another family, so that one of us could take my son home to bed and the other could stay and serve the needs of the community (consultation, clean-up, providing rides, etc.).

Somehow there is always a balance to maintain but nonetheless one based upon spiritual principles!

Irene Dominguez The most important thing is to attend to spiritual matters. If they had too much homework, we helped them before and/or after Feast.

Michelle Sharpe We have always gone to Feast and worked out the homework. In some cases we would leave Feast a little earlier. We'd have some food at the social part and carry our desserts home. We would get up earlier the following morning and finish any homework. Another way was to remind the children about Feast beforehand, that way they could organize ahead of time. They were very good about this, other than the fact that they would often be quite tired.

Linda Paulson Feast and Holy Day celebrations always took precedence over homework or anything else. They were always required to attend the devotional portion and they were excused for the administrative and social portions. If there was something that they wanted to bring up during the administrative portion, they could do that first and then be excused from the remainder.

Lucy Matthews When it was time for final exams and similar important deadlines, that took precedence. We're supposed to be outstanding. The schools are not set up to coordinate with Bahá'í Feasts. We feel that there are times when schoolwork just has to come first. It would be good for the parents to have a small Feast at home for the children.

Tanya Charles So far, schoolwork has not interfered with Bahá'í activities. I do let the kids know about the schedule for the day each morning, even further in advance if there is something that will have a major impact, such as missing school later in the week for a Holy Day. On the night of a Feast, with school the next day, the younger two can complete their work early, before dinner. Our eighth-grader can't complete her homework before dinner and usually has to stay up a bit late that night to finish. Of course, the younger two are up late, too, by the time we attend Feast and drive home. We find this workable. So far!

One year, when our oldest was little, we never managed to attend Feast at all. Feast began after her bedtime and we lived quite a long way away. We held our own Feasts that year.

Some acceptable reasons to miss Feast: a school commitment such as a band performance, a school play performance, a game or finals. If your child has signed up for a class such as band, chorus or an extracurricular activity such as a play or sports, those are commitments to be honoured. It helps me to think of my kids' school as their work. Some commitments are obligations that must be kept. Some are more flexible. Which commitment would you keep if it were you and your job? Try to translate that for your children.

Also, some Baháʼí events are more important to me. I'd rather miss a Feast than the Riḍván or Naw-Rúz observances. If sports practice or play rehearsal is on the night of, say, the first day of Riḍván observance, can you contact the teacher and negotiate skipping this once or leaving early? On occasions that we do miss the community Feast or Holy Day, we hold our own. Missing these events entirely can often be avoided. Be creative!

Farzaneh Knight Their studies took precedence but we encouraged them firmly to plan their homework so they *could* attend Feast. They were also encouraged to host Feast at least once a year and to contribute to the fund.

Julie Young Our children were never allowed to skip Feast because of school.

Simon Scott Yes, there are times that I would allow them to skip Feast because of school or workload. Were I to force them and create a burdensome approach to attending a function, then that sets up more resistance in the future. The key to me is that they feel the need for personal spiritual transformation exemplifying the best examples given by Baháʼuʼlláh and ʻAbduʼl-Bahá. For me, that supersedes the requirement to attend any single Baháʼí function.

Did your child ever not want to attend Feast, children's classes or some other Baháʼí event?

Since children of Baháʼí parents are considered to be Baháʼís, they are to be encouraged to attend all Feasts, there to share the reading of the Writings and prayers and be bathed in the spirit of the community. It is the hope of the House of Justice that every Feast will be a feast of love when the children will give and receive the tangible affection of the community and its individual members.[3]

... children should be trained to understand the spiritual significance of the gatherings of the followers of the Blessed Beauty, and to appreciate the honour and bounty of being able to take part in them, whatever their outward form may be.[4]

Edyth Lewis When the children were small they eagerly went to Feasts, children's classes and Bahá'í events. It was only as they grew older that they resisted going to children's classes.

I can remember taking one of my sons, at the age of ten, kicking and screaming to the children's Sunday classes. I would have left him at home had there been someone to look after him. At that time my husband was an Auxiliary Board member and was frequently away at weekends. I was one of the Sunday school teachers and so could not opt out. My son is marginally dyslexic and struggled to keep up with the class. Often his teacher, who was not trained, would say, 'Is that the best you can do?', little realizing that the answer was probably 'yes'. The only times that he did not mind coming was on the odd occasions when I was taking his class because I knew what he was capable of and could play to his strengths.

He also felt that the other children all knew each other (this was true – they were all related) and he came into the group as an outsider. There was little point of contact as his interests appeared very different from theirs.

The Universal House of Justice has put emphasis on the importance of children's classes, making it one of the core activities. It is important that children feel comfortable in and with the classes they attend otherwise they will resent them and in turn the Faith. Sometimes we lose sight of the goal which is surely to bring a soul nearer to its Creator. If a child is resisting attendance then the parents need to look closely at the reason. If the classes prevent him from doing something else that he loves – e.g. playing for the school football team – can they be at a different time? If he doesn't have any friends among the children in the class, can the parents either invite some of the classmates over so that he can make friends with them outside the class or invite some of his non-Bahá'í friends to attend now that the classes are 'open to all'?

DEVELOPING A LOVE FOR THE FAITH

Are the classes too easy, too hard or just plain boring? If so, then the parents need to speak to the teacher and possibly arrange for their child to attend a different class.

Attendance at the old style classes used to drop off at around the age of 12. This was not only true of my own children but of their peers. Teenagers need a lot of sleep and to get them up on a Sunday to attend the classes was a big challenge. They resented having to go to 'school' at the weekend. Now with youth and junior youth study circles which take this age group away from the classroom there is scope for teenagers to have a Sunday morning lie-in and attend classes that don't feel anything like school.

Julie Young At any given time, there were things that they did not want to go to. There were other things that they *also* wanted to go to. This was nothing against the Bahá'í function; there were just competing events. We had to do things to assist our children to understand that Bahá'í functions take priority. We reminded them beforehand. We as parents have the responsibility to assist them in making the correct decision and to enable them to feel good about Bahá'í events. We would ask them if there was a conflict in their calendar. When it came to Feast, going to the devotionals at least was better than not going at all.

Our son did not want to attend Feast one evening, simply because he did not feel like it. This was unacceptable to us. I told him that he must attend and explained to him that if I were to die that night, I would be held accountable for his not attending Feast. He attended! We did not have that problem again.

In small communities, a lot of children will fall into this rut, where they don't want to attend Bahá'í functions because they have no peers. It is important to explain to them that this is between you as the parents and God and that these are the things that we have to do. We have to instil obedience from the very beginning. From the time that they are young, we should share the writings on obedience with them. Show them models and examples of obedience. We should also model obedience to our own parents. We should show our children that even as adults we are obedient.

Celia Stewart We told her that we were responsible for her spiritual welfare until she was 15 years old and after that she could make her own decisions. After she was 15 we would invite her to Bahá'í functions but we didn't nag.

Katayun Golshani When children say that they don't want to do something, it's usually because it's not emotionally attractive to them. When we look directly to the parents, we see that the child is really reacting to their communication and emotional expressions. The parents themselves may not want to go to Feast. They may be uptight, tense or tired. That's the first thing that parents need to tune into. What kind of attitude am I creating about Feasts and Bahá'í events?

Then when we attend Feast, we need to look at the kind of emotional experiences that children have there. Is everybody friendly towards them? Are they feeling loved? Do they feel welcomed? Do they feel shunned? Many of the friends could inadvertently be sending messages to the child that he is a nuisance. To me, saying that the child is only two and cannot attend Feast is not acceptable.

Children can very gradually be accustomed and conditioned to sit and listen at Feast for longer and longer periods of time. Young children can't do that.

The solution is for the parents to make *every* effort to prepare the child before going, feed him, be relaxed, be loving and be cheerful. The parents need to be excited themselves.

I have never seen a child who has felt loved and whose parents were vigilant about creating the right atmosphere and attitudes not want to attend Feast. I remember telling my children that if you want to attend Feast, you have to do X, Y and Z. They would go to any lengths to do whatever I asked them to do in order to be able to attend.

When a child says that he does not want to attend something, he is reacting to an emotional experience. Perhaps he feels shunned or excluded from a certain group. Parents need to find out what kind of emotional experience the child has had that caused this. They then need to correct it.

DEVELOPING A LOVE FOR THE FAITH

Simon Scott Yes, there have been many times that they might not want to attend a function. When they were little children, they went if I went, even if they did not want to attend. Now that they are teenagers, I do not force them as I feel the individual needs to have an innate desire to be part of Baháʼuʼlláh. However, at the same time, I have always wanted to know the reason for any reluctance to attend a Baháʼí function. If it is a result of 'Feast is boring', then that tells me that adult Baháʼís need to give serious consideration to adapting presentations so that they are not boring but have some benefit and create a positive feeling in the child for having attended. The question here would be, what is the reason why the child would not want to participate?

Todd and Debbie McEwen The situation has rarely arisen. When there is an event at which we feel the arrangements for children are inadequate or unsuitable, we will not take them – sometimes doing something by ourselves instead or sometimes one of us has gone and the other stayed behind with the children. We feel that it is wrong to take children along to an event at which there is nothing suitable for them and believe that this is likely to put them off the Baháʼí Faith rather than encourage them. Encouragement is better than coercion.

Paul Oliver I don't remember this happening. But I expect there was some resistance at some time. However, it was just what we did as a family (like sitting around a table eating dinner). There was not an option to sit at home if you felt like it. It was part of the definition of our family life.

Richard and Theresa Baker Yes, often! It was fine when there were children of their own age at a Feast or other Baháʼí activity but when this wasn't the case, they found the Feast boring and didn't want to come along. We understood this situation. Sometimes one or the other of us would go to the Feast and the other would stay at home with the children. We didn't think it fair to take them along knowing that they wouldn't get anything out of it. Other times we would explain the importance of attending the Feast. However, we thought it important to maintain family unity and not to overreact when they didn't want to go. We had come across Bahá'í families where children were made to go to a Feast and, as a result, the children became rebellious.

Linda Paulson When the children were younger we always arranged to have a treat for the social portion of Feast or during the Holy Day celebrations. This helped to motivate the children to look forward to attending such events. When the children were older – during the pre-teen and early teen years – they would have preferred to do other things, whether it was to watch television, read a book or play with friends. If we couldn't reason with them, we would invoke our parental authority and insist they attend. They would usually be disgruntled through the first few prayers but within five minutes or so they would relax and enjoy the activities.

What advice would you give to Bahá'í parents living in isolated communities where there are few or no other Bahá'ís?

Look ye not upon the fewness of thy numbers, rather, seek ye out hearts that are pure. One consecrated soul is preferable to a thousand other souls. If a small number of people gather lovingly together, with absolute purity and sanctity, with their hearts free of the world, experiencing the emotions of the Kingdom and the powerful magnetic forces of the Divine, and being at one in their happy fellowship, that gathering will exert its influence over all the earth. The nature of that band of people, the words they speak, the deeds they do, will unleash the bestowals of Heaven, and provide a foretaste of eternal bliss. The hosts of the Company on high will defend them, and the angels of the Abhá Paradise, in continuous succession, will come down to their aid.[5]

Andrew Adams The spiritual life inside the family is most important. The community situation will work itself out. Don't expect

DEVELOPING A LOVE FOR THE FAITH

the community to raise your child. If you want your child to be firm in the Faith, you must create conditions at home to make that happen. You have to teach that child its spiritual responsibilities. Pray with him, read the writings with him, experience the joy of your Faith together.

George and Mary Burke We would encourage Bahá'í parents who live in isolated communities to do two very important things. First, teach the Faith in your home by having regular firesides. This will help instil a Bahá'í identity in your children.

Second, travel to other areas as much as possible to give your children exposure to other areas and cultures as well as to other Bahá'ís.

Farzaneh Knight Keep the flame of the Faith strong in the home.

- Celebrate the 19 Day Feasts and the Holy Days, and particularly Ayyám-i-Há. Make the Holy Days somehow special. Serve the children their favourite foods. Make them memorable.
- Play Bahá'í CDs for them to fall asleep to.
- Watch Bahá'í videos such as *Bahá'í Newsreel*.
- Take them to events where there are other Bahá'ís their own age, such as summer schools. Even if this is only done once a year, this will help them to have warm feelings towards the Faith. They will *live* for that encounter the following year. Now with email, they can create life-long friendships and lifelines.
- Read them stories of heroes and heroines of the Faith. Tell your children that they can become like them one day.

Living in a large community does not guarantee anything without all of these efforts too!

Margerie Gibson This is the situation we have been in ourselves. Our daughter is the *only* Bahá'í child her age in this area. The others are pre-schoolers or teens, neither of whom have much interest in a nine year old. We try to build as much of a relationship as possible with the other Baháʼís by placing a special focus on the social aspect. We plan monthly ice cream socials in the summertime, where we invite Baháʼís and non-Baháʼís alike. We have game nights in the winter months. We try to invite the friends over for meals at least once every Gregorian month.

Angela Brown I've noticed that there do not seem to be any particular prayers revealed for the sole purpose of helping us become better parents. I have come to the conclusion that Baháʼu'lláh wants us to read *all* of the prayers so that we can become better parents! That is, the more we pray and beg for assistance and make the effort to become better Baháʼís, the greater the chance that we will become better parents.

Yet applying all this may be difficult for some who are isolated from any form of Baháʼí community life. It therefore becomes urgent to surround the child with reflections of the spiritual principles, with the Master's photo framed beautifully, with the Greatest Name over the door, with illuminated quotations and posters illustrating the principles. Many children's books with both specific Baháʼí stories and indirect stories that teach a Baháʼí principle can be shared, along with videos, CDs and even computer software.

But for children nothing is more important than their immersion in the company of Baháʼís. This is probably one of the reasons why the Guardian emphasized the importance of planning vacations and holidays to coincide with sessions at Baháʼí summer schools. Many Baháʼí children remember these blessed and joyous days, however few in number, above all of the other days of the school year! My older daughters went to Green Acre Baháʼí school every summer, while our youngest went to Louis Gregory Baháʼí Institute every time there was a children's weekend or a summer or winter school.

There are also teaching trips. It is part of a Baháʼí family's experience to go on teaching trips from time to time. I took turns taking my older children with me on teaching trips and to conferences outside our locality. Otherwise they all accompanied me to migrant camps to teach the Faith and help with consolidation. I really believe that these are among the best ways to prevent the development of an isolation mentality. We are so connected now and we can pray to convey to our children the identity of pioneers rather than Bahá'ís who are separated from all others. But it will take work and sacrifice so that we don't allow ourselves to feel isolated.

We also need to constantly refer to the Bahá'í calendar – to the 19 Day Feasts and the Holy Days. Holy Days can be commemorated as though an entire Bahá'í community were present. We can invite Bahá'ís to travel teach to our locality to help with all these.

We make an effort to drive an hour or so to get our son to a Sunday morning Bahá'í spiritual programme in a neighbouring community. We also have him give talks at our small family Feasts, which he is asked on occasion to host.

Though we visit churches from time to time and share the Tablet to the Christians, we let him know that we are doing so because Bahá'u'lláh told us to 'Consort with the followers of all religions in a spirit of friendliness and fellowship'.[6]

Phoebe Untekar Make any necessary sacrifice to take your children regularly to Bahá'í summer schools, conferences and children's classes. We were the only Bahá'ís in our town for many years and afterwards there was only a small community. My kids have often told me how important Green Lake and Camp Byron Bahá'í conferences were for them, especially as they began to struggle with pre-teen issues. The friendships they formed there have been sustained until today.

Edyth Lewis If possible, take them to a Bahá'í summer school each year so that they can meet up with other children.

Try to pair up with another Bahá'í family that has children of a similar age, even if these are fairly far away and can only be contacted by email or phone. I feel it is important that children have

Bahá'í friends. When we were pioneering we were lucky in that there was another Bahá'í family who had children of a similar age and we often did things together, like going to the beach.

Subscribe to *Brilliant Star* and/or *Dayspring*. When they arrive, go through these with your children. Make it an exciting event – something to be anticipated.

Make sure that they have a good Bahá'í library. There are a number of workbooks that have been produced over the years and these are a good way to talk about the Faith with children.

Tanya Charles A small community can be a wonderful advantage for young ones who feel truly known and loved by all. Even the members of a community whom other adults find challenging are usually wonderful to the children. However, being truly isolated can be a real test. My advice: Be sure your kids get everything you want them to have spiritually speaking, even if it means you have to do it! You may host every Feast, teach children's classes and orchestrate every Holy Day. This is a great and vital place to put your energy! Be reasonable, though. Having children's classes every other week can be enough, especially if you are trying to balance other time-consuming administrative work or have a demanding job.

Find good resources. Having good Bahá'í books for children or a subscription to a nice Bahá'í magazine is a great way to fit in more teaching time while strengthening your child's sense of Bahá'í identity at the same time.

Also, if you have the chance to attend Bahá'í schools or conferences, that can be a treat for all, you included.

As your children get older, include them more and more. With your help, they can host one of the portions of Feast from the time they are five or six years old. They can host the whole event a little later. They can go with you as you teach or help prepare the fireside you host.

I think it's hardest for our youth to be isolated Bahá'ís. They put such value in the opinions of their peers and want to spend more and more time with them rather than with the family. Youth groups can be Bahá'í youth groups with most of the participants being non-Bahá'ís. Once again, get information about what someone else has prepared if you feel overwhelmed at the idea of starting from scratch. The investment in the youth is sure to pay big dividends!

Irene Dominguez Parents should start their own children's classes for their children and they can invite other children and neighbours.

Lucy Matthews That's how I grew up and how a lot of other Bahá'ís still grow up. My mother was really the only Bahá'í in Lima, Ohio, until my great-grandmother came (who was one of the early American Bahá'ís). Every now and then, my mother, younger brother and I would have these cosy times where we'd sit down on the floor. She'd tell us stories. We'd say a prayer. It was just a very special time with mommy. Our connection to the Bahá'í Faith was, 'Oh, these are the best times!' and we really treasured them. Mother showed us how much she loved us and we were all together. It was such fun. We were not aware of being taught. We would talk about stories and how to respond to different situations. It was very casual. Every night at bedtime, we would pray, read a Hidden Word and talk about that Hidden Word.

How can we increase Bahá'í influence for our children in an isolated community?

Lucy Matthews At the Bahá'í Sunday school when I was growing up in Ohio, a lot of the children who attended were not from Bahá'í families. The parents liked our approach and the openness with which we were taught. They liked the fact that their children were taught more than they were taught in a Christian Sunday school. The parents were invited to send their children if they wished. The children liked the Bahá'í Sunday school much more. You can simply open the Sunday school. If there are no other children and no community, it's up to the parents to make sure that they have a very cosy time so that the children can have a very loving and happy experience, so that they can think, 'This is a special time with mommy' or 'a special time with daddy'. They should feel warm, protected, loved and happy.

Melissa Taheri By example and a close family. Children need to see the things that are important to parents such as prayer, fasting, attending Feasts, observing Holy Days and how parents handle situations such as being served alcohol.

Margerie Gibson We keep a calendar for her to fill in every evening at sunset (the beginning of the Bahá'í day) with the Bahá'í day and date. I made up the calendar blank on the computer and at the beginning of each Bahá'í month she fills in the Bahá'í month name, the English translation, the numeric order of that month (1st, 2nd, etc.), and the Bahá'í year in spaces at the top of the page, then fills in the date daily at sunset or soon after. We also have a calendar done the same way for the Christian calendar and she fills it in at the same time. This gives a daily reinforcement to the priority of the Bahá'í order of life, keeps her aware of when Feast will be (on the first of the month) and so on.

Also, when she was just a baby, I had her with me when saying my obligatory prayers. As she got older, she would do ablutions with me and hold my hand as I recited the noon prayer. She had the prayer memorized by the time she was four years old. She now has her own set of prayer beads for her daily recitation of Alláh-u-Abhá as well.

She also loves to listen to music based on Bahá'í scriptures. She practises her handwriting by copying Bahá'í scriptures.

Having these daily rhythms is crucial to creating a Bahá'í identity in children, even ones living in a large community!

Todd and Debbie McEwen Spend time with other Bahá'ís when you can. Invite them to visit you and go and visit them. Encourage the use of email to Bahá'í friends. Go to summer schools and other

Baháʼí gatherings, if and when you can. As they get older, encourage them to go to Baháʼí youth events.

Linda Bandari We can increase Baháʼí influence on children who live in an isolated community by bringing them to events in a nearby community whenever possible, by inviting Baháʼís to our community to give a fireside or for a special event, attending Baháʼí conferences, subscribing to a Baháʼí magazine for children such as *Brilliant Star*, doing something special for Holy Days that our children can participate in, reading Baháʼí books to our children and discussing them, and by holding Baháʼí classes for our children.

Richard and Theresa Baker Try and invite Baháʼís to your home and make sure the children are involved in family activities at the time. Also be prepared to drive the children to Baháʼí schools and other Baháʼí activities such as conferences and weekend schools.

Irene Dominguez When the parents go teaching, they should take their children with them. Prayer should be a central focus, as well as reading Baháʼí stories together.

Simon Scott The greatest influence anyone has on their children is that of example. 'Let deeds, not words, be your adorning.'[7]

How can we define Baháʼí identity for our children?

It is often difficult for us to do things because they are so very different from what we are used to, not because the thing itself is particularly difficult. With you, and indeed most Baháʼís, who are now, as adults, accepting this glorious Faith, no doubt some of the ordinances, like fasting and daily prayer, are hard to understand and obey at first. But we must always think that these things are given to all men for a thousand years to come. For Baháʼí children who see these things practised in the home, they will be as natural and necessary a thing as going to church on Sunday was to the more pious generation of Christians. Bahá'u'lláh would not have given us these things if they would not greatly benefit us, and, like children who are sensible enough to realize their father is wise and does what is good for them, we must accept to obey these ordinances even though at first we may not see any need for them. As we obey them we will gradually come to see in ourselves the benefits they confer.[8]

Julie Young By following the Bahá'í calendar, attending the Feasts and Holy Days. *Nothing* is more important than that. Their lives should be scheduled around that. They have to know and be told about these events in advance, not at the last minute. *Nothing* is more important than their spiritual growth, not their grades or anything else (although my children had excellent grades too). Their lives should be framed around the Bahá'í calendar.

Donna Smith By being Bahá'ís ourselves and by putting our children first, even sometimes before Bahá'í work. Many children are lost to the Faith because their parents are busy serving the Cause and hope that God will provide somehow. He doesn't. We are serving the Faith when we put our children's needs first.

Donald Pope Through the use of stories, explain their station and model a trust in the ever-present God. Show them what they were given. Show them by your actions and your treatment of them that to whom much is given, from him is much expected. And be sure to give them much – understanding, love, respect and encouragement. Always acknowledge any success as well as mentioning any shortcoming.

Marva Ross Take the whole family to a Bahá'í summer school every summer. This way, everyone can experience the Bahá'í way of life and see the practice of Bahá'í ideals before their eyes. It's also very helpful to associate closely with a few other families who share your values and ideals.

DEVELOPING A LOVE FOR THE FAITH

Celia Stewart The sweetest display of 'Bahá'í identity' I have ever seen in my children is when my oldest was playing with her playhouse. She was lying on her tummy and arranging the furniture and moving the people around. I asked her what they were doing and she said, 'Getting ready for Feast!' She was about three years old. Now that the kids are older, they discuss the way the Faith influences their decision-making. We have always been in areas with few youth, pretty much only our own children. It is hard on them in some ways. Keturah loved being in Haifa with all the other youth – and suddenly felt the joy of being with kindred spirits. I think the best way for children to be taught Bahá'í identity is for the parents to have a strong Bahá'í identity.

Did you celebrate Christmas? If not, how did you handle not celebrating it?

As regards the celebration of the Christian Holiday by the believers; it is surely preferable and even highly advisable that the friends should in their relation to each other discontinue observing such holidays as Christmas and New Years, and to have their festival gatherings of this nature instead during the Intercalary Days and Naw-Rúz.[9]

Donna Smith We became Bahá'ís when our oldest children were two and four. We continued to celebrate Christmas but on a descending scale. We preferred to emphasize the true story of Christ's birth. We warned them each year that we would be stopping and by the time they were seven and nine they only received one present each from us. All decorations were gone from the house after that. We did this slowly on purpose. It didn't feel fair to the children to make a blunt change that they wouldn't understand. But by the time they were seven and nine they were able to understand and could also look forward to Ayyám-i-Há. They also began to look forward to the Fast, by trying to give up a cookie a day. If they didn't succeed, there was no problem, they were just practising for the big day when they could really fast. Kids love to imitate their parents. Our third son was born when our second son was seven. Our third son never celebrated Christmas. Of course we honoured our Christian parents and gave gifts to them. On Christmas day, we visited with grandparents who gave the children gifts but at home it was just another quiet day. They understood. None of them experienced any trauma. They are all Bahá'ís, married to Bahá'ís, and are raising their children as Bahá'ís.

Celia Stewart We celebrate the spiritual aspect of the birth of Christ. We have never had a tree or any of the trappings of Christmas but we would take walks to the chapel nearby and look at the Nativity scene and talk about the birth of Jesus. On Christmas morning we would walk down and see the baby in the manger. We have a nice dinner on Christmas afternoon and read from the Bible. The children would receive a few gifts from non-Bahá'í relatives. The kids would open the gifts after dinner. Christmas is always a very relaxing day! None of our kids are bothered by not celebrating Christmas. They go to school parties or friends' parties and exchange gifts. We don't prohibit any celebration like some other religionists do.

Irene Dominguez We did not celebrate Christmas. We placed a great emphasis on Naw-Rúz and made that very important – new clothes and a big celebration. We also gave gifts during each of the days of Ayyám-i-Há.

John and Barbara Hartley We never celebrated Christmas as a family because we were married as Bahá'ís. We sometimes took part in our extended family's Christmas celebrations. To counter the effect of Christmas, we made a 'big deal' out of Intercalary Days. We had a present for each person in the family and had a specific time when we opened the present for the day. We always had friends in for dinner on one or two of those days. We decorated our place (and still do) for the celebrations.

DEVELOPING A LOVE FOR THE FAITH

Phoebe Untekar We never celebrated Christmas in our own home or put up any decorations. We spent Christmas eve with my husband's family and Christmas day with my parents. Our kids gave and received many gifts, so they didn't feel left out among their friends. We made Ayyám-i-Há a very special time, took treats to school and exchanged gifts in our family and with my mom, who is also a Bahá'í. Our children never felt deprived, although they were aware of being different.

Bernice McKenzie We celebrated Christmas once when we lived in North America to please the grandparents. When we pioneered, we did not celebrate any Christian holidays. When the children were young (around five or six) and wondered why we didn't have a Christmas tree and other decorations, we would simply state that Christmas was only for one day and as Bahá'ís we get four and sometimes five days of gift-giving and celebration. They bought it hook, line and sinker. I remember one time for the Intercalary Days we borrowed a tree from one of their friends and decorated it like a Christmas tree. My daughter's last Intercalary Days was a wonderful occasion. We arranged to have the local balloon people make up a balloon tree and that was our Intercalary Day tree.

I think the way we handled not celebrating Christmas was that, bottom-line, we are Bahá'ís. Bahá'ís have their own special days. End of story.

Katayun Golshani With everything that parents do, they need to ask themselves, 'What kind of a meaning and what kind of a conclusion are we communicating to our children?' If I celebrate a religious holiday without having any kind of emotional or mental belief system, for no legitimate reason other than for the materialistic aspects or for fear of being different or because everyone else is and so on – you are teaching the message to your child that you do things in life that you don't believe in, that you place emphasis on the materialistic aspect of something and that you lack the courage to do what you believe you should do. You're showing your children to do something simply because everyone else is. If the parents set up a Christmas tree and do the whole Christmas thing, the child is going to have an emotional tie with the event. That is not in congruence with the practice of a Bahá'í life. It's not going in the same direction. If you want to decorate your house in the winter, there are so many other options of decorating it then! Having a Christmas tree is not the only option. Why not decorate your house with a Bahá'í theme – such as activities, singing prayers, telling stories about the Central Figures and how they related to different religions, teaching progressive revelation? By doing this we are taking away the meaningless celebration of it and elevating it by showing how our Bahá'í Faith relates to other faiths.

I don't see anything wrong with joining non-Bahá'í family members and supporting them in their religious holidays.

Farzaneh Knight We negotiated. Four days of Ayyám-i-Há and one day of Naw-Rúz versus one day of Christmas. Guess what won? More gifts! One of our daughters decided at the age of seven that she wanted to become a Christian. I said, 'Fine. No problem. You can get one Christmas present and no presents for Ayyám-i-Há and Naw-Rúz, since those are special Bahá'í days.' After thinking it over, she said, 'Mommy, I've always been a Bahá'í. I was just joking.' When friends would ask them what they got for Christmas, they left them wide-eyed with the 5:1 explanation. It got to the point that by the time they were 15 and 16 their friends were celebrating Ayyám-i-Há with them in school. They were baking cakes and making sweets for the entire class.

Michelle Sharpe We have been Bahá'ís for six years. We were still attached to Christmas in the first year. We bought a large plant that we later placed in the garden. We decorated this plant with symbols of all religions. It was fun. Everyone got one gift. The following year we did not do the plant routine. We only did gifts. In the third year, we did not celebrate. So it has evolved. I have noticed that as the children are getting older, they are talking more and more about Christmas. As communities and as families, we need to make Ayyám-i-Há very special.

DEVELOPING A LOVE FOR THE FAITH

Margerie Gibson Absolutely *not!* The beloved Guardian is *very* clear about that. The only thing we do at Christmas is to set up a Nativity scene on a chest sitting on one side of the living room, in honour of Jesus Christ's birth, because we do believe in His revelation. We do not decorate our home with greenery or lights, exchange gifts or any other of the traditional American modes of celebration. We set up the Nativity as a sign to our Christian friends that we believe in Jesus. It is used more as a teaching tool than a holiday decoration. We also study the Jewish holidays year round and may have a menorah or a dreidel sitting around at certain times as well.

We do have relatives who are Christian, so we visit our parents a couple of weeks before Christmas and help them get ready for Christmas by decorating their tree for them and putting up the other decorations. We treat it as a service project for Grandma because her health is not good and she is unable to do the decorating herself anymore and I love doing things for her! We also go down to their house early on Christmas day and help Grandma again by getting the Christmas dinner put together as much as possible before the other relatives arrive. This way they get to enjoy their Christmas celebration and we get to be of service.

If we didn't have so many close friends who were strongly Christian, we wouldn't put out the Nativity set; and once our parents pass away, we will stop 'celebrating' Christmas completely.

What would you do if your child were approaching the age of maturity and said that she did not wish to be a Bahá'í?

The age of maturity has been set by Bahá'u'lláh at 15 years. This is the age at which a person is expected to obey the laws of the *Kitáb-i-Aqdas* in regard to prayer, fasting, marriage, etc. Children of Bahá'í parents under the age of 15 are considered to be Bahá'ís.

Lucy Matthews When our daughter was about seven years old she went through a period when she told me firmly that there was no such thing as God. She was adamant about it. I told her that I thought that she would find that there is a God. I didn't make a big issue out of it. I listened and said that it was interesting. I was both amused and a little worried. I figured that it would straighten out. I said, 'Well, I like to say prayers.' She would go along with prayers and saying the Hidden Words but she wasn't too happy about it. We'd go to the public library and get some books. And one book in particular – an Irish tale – touched her heart. All of a sudden she realized the significance of prayer and wanted to pray. She then believed in God.

If my child were approaching the age of maturity and said that she did not wish to be a Bahá'í, I would have to accept it. We have to start very early. I can see how children may not wish to be Bahá'ís because that means that they have to be different. A lot of my Bahá'í friends who grew up with me are Bahá'ís because we all attended summer schools. We had special youth sessions. It's very important that kids attend these summer schools. They then have a Bahá'í identity. They develop close personal Bahá'í friendships that will last all their lives. You can't wait until the kids are almost 15 to start that. You have to start this early. The community needs to have junior youth activities. We had them in my house because we had a big party room. The youth can take care of them and teach them something. We supplied the refreshments. They did the rest. They needed people that they could relate to much better. They didn't want to listen to some 'old fuddies'! The community needs to see to it that the youth and junior youth get together. They need a social and spiritual atmosphere. If you leave it all to the youth, they'll go overboard and have all social. If you leave it all to the older Bahá'ís, it'll go in the other direction and be only studying. You need a balance. But summer schools are the most important thing. The kids love them.

Tanya Charles This is a big one! Please, please, resist all temptation to react emotionally to this bombshell (from your perspective). How can this be? Where did I go wrong? What are you thinking? This is your soul at stake. This is a critical time to listen. If you

DEVELOPING A LOVE FOR THE FAITH

were able to compose yourself and say, 'Wow, really? I'd like to hear more about this', that would be a great response, in my opinion. Youth need a safe sounding board, and if it's not the family, it is the friends. By saying things, thinking things, doing things, they get to try them on, so to speak. It's great if they can do some of this trying on and exploring with us, the parents. So, hold on to your hat – and your tongue! And listen to the concerns your child has. Don't try to answer them right now. Just listen. If some truly concern you, tuck the thought away or even say, 'I'd like to study more about that thought.' But let it go for now. This isn't the moment to pull out the books and 'prove' the Faith to your child. This is the moment to be an active listener. Repeat back what you hear your child say. 'So you feel that the fact that we don't have women on the Universal House of Justice shows that we don't really live the principle of equality of men and women. I see.' Honestly, letting your child express herself may be enough. Haven't we all had ideas that, once aired in the light of day, suddenly don't make sense?

When your youth has shared all of her thoughts and you have repeated each of them, end the discussion. Don't reply now. Hugs are fine. A plan to talk about this again in a few days is fine. A plan to study more is fine. But let this end without 'fixing' it.

Now you can go to work, pray, study, involve family members or community support. Without anyone the wiser, the next Feast readings (if your child still attends Feast) might reflect one of your child's concerns. Or family prayers could nonchalantly refer to them. Or you can seriously plan to study every Sunday for 30 minutes with your youth about the concerns, as fellow students seeking the truth together, rather than you informing your child of the truth.

Ultimately, no one can make anyone else a Bahá'í. We may, in fact, have children who grow up and do not choose to be Bahá'ís. But if we try to force them to be Bahá'ís we run the risk of chasing them out of the Faith.

Michelle Sharpe I would listen very carefully to the reasons. I would not pressure the child. I would ask her to explore other religions by reading the holy books and thereby make comparisons.

Simon Scott The choice of becoming a Bahá'í is purely up to the individual. However, I am unwilling to let one of my children just disregard Bahá'u'lláh. If you seek out and study the earliest days of the Bahá'ís in America and the West, you will find that they were frequently taught that Bahá'u'lláh was the 'return' of Jesus and, as such, once an individual understood this, it was his obligation to accept Bahá'u'lláh. As a result, oftentimes entire families ended up petitioning 'Abdu'l-Bahá to become Bahá'ís. Bahá'u'lláh is the only solution to the world's problems and I would very much try to articulate that to anyone who did not want to 'declare'. If they truly did not believe this to be true, as opposed to an incomplete understanding of what being a Bahá'í means, then they would be free not to be a Bahá'í.

Unfortunately, I have seen far too many examples of people carrying Bahá'í cards who didn't want to be Bahá'ís or participate as Bahá'ís or even did not know much about Bahá'u'lláh. A religion does not spread successfully with that kind of membership.

Angela Brown This happened with our oldest daughter, who didn't wish to commit herself to the Faith when she was 15, though the signs began to appear when she was 12. It was then that she began to be sullen on the subject of Bahá'í life and practice as she was drawn into the social world to which she was so attracted.

I don't know whether such a child could be called a 'problem child', as mentioned by Shoghi Effendi in response to a letter from a concerned parent about her child who seemed to be turning away from participation in the Bahá'í community. However, the Guardian's advice was to be loving and patient, not to force the child to participate in Bahá'í events, and that eventually the child would on her own overcome the obstacles within herself.[10]

I tried to follow this advice, though at times it seemed very difficult and distressing. Finally, when she was 18, she found herself joining a teaching project of her own accord and responding to another adult Bahá'í's invitation to make her declaration of faith. After doing so, she regretted that she had lost some of the most significant years of her life functioning as though she were not a

DEVELOPING A LOVE FOR THE FAITH

Baháʼí youth! Yet this was her own decision in both cases. Now she is a wonderful and devoted Baháʼí.

Another daughter announced when she was 14 that she really didn't even believe in God – to our shock and horror. After all, we had been having family prayers daily all of her life! She went through quite a few difficulties in her own relationship with God and Baháʼu'lláh but she too is a very devoted Baháʼí now, having gone on a year of service to India and having worked through her own spiritual difficulties.

I now believe that each person (even a Baháʼí child) will come to a point in his life when his faith must be tested in order for him to be able to hear the call of the Beloved and to rise and serve, and each will do this in his own way.

Margerie Gibson Respect her decision, and pray! I'm sure we would also ask her to explain why she makes this choice and afterwards try to be an example to lead her back to the Faith.

Beth Bishop One would have to respect them but I would try to see why they said this and show them that the teachings of Baháʼu'lláh are the most reasonable viewpoint and the best chance for the world. Many children say this when they are 13 or so and later change their mind. So I would not treat it as final at this age. My eldest son is a Baháʼí but since he started university he has not attended events unless they're held at our house when he is here. There is not much one can do except pray and encourage them to make the right choices.

Paul Oliver I am so grateful that in the US, with children's registration, that at least the youth have to deliberately decide *not* to be a Baháʼí rather than decide to be one. Both children had their period of doubt, part of which was the natural rebellion against us as parents. We told them that doubt was natural. And that this was the most important decision of their lives, having to do with their souls. We told them that we loved and supported them and tried to give them the tools to make an informed choice. We then stepped back and let their struggle be between them and Bahá'u'lláh, not with us. It would have been difficult if either child had specifically said that he or she wanted to resign from the Faith. But I would have struggled to support it.

I'll never forget how my 15 year old daughter, when in the garden at Bahjí while on pilgrimage, broke down in tears and told me how she didn't believe that she belonged there. She did not feel what she thought she should be feeling. I listened a lot, shared some prayers and passages with her and told her that part of the spiritual path is feeling distance and separation from God and that God is always with her.

Edyth Lewis This happened to us with one of our sons. It is not the end of the earth! We never felt that we had 'failed' with him, although he did like being the 'black sheep' of the family. We could always see the good side of him and we tried not to make an issue of his not being a Bahá'í. Of course we always prayed for him, talked to him but accepted that once he had reached maturity, his soul was his own responsibility.

Some of those who are brought up as Bahá'ís need to feel what it is like not to be a Bahá'í in order to truly claim that being a Bahá'í is their own decision and not something that they have done to please their parents.

Andrew Adams I would seek to ascertain whether the child was sincere in stating he did not want to join the Bahá'í community. If sincere, I would seek to understand his feelings. I would seek to assist him to overcome his difficulties. In my mind, he is already a Bahá'í, having grown up in the Faith.

2

Teaching Your Child the Principle of Obedience

How did you punish your child? Were privileges withdrawn? Did you give time-outs or did you sometimes prefer to ignore the bad behaviour?

Discipline of some sort, whether physical, moral or intellectual, is indeed indispensable, and no training can be said to be complete and fruitful if it disregards this element. The child when born is far from being perfect. It is not only helpless, but actually is imperfect, and even is naturally inclined towards evil. He should be trained, his natural inclinations harmonized, adjusted and controlled, and if necessary suppressed or regulated, so as to ensure his healthy physical and moral development. Bahá'í parents cannot simply adopt an attitude of non-resistance towards their children, particularly those who are unruly and violent by nature. It is not even sufficient that they should pray on their behalf. Rather they should endeavour to inculcate, gently and patiently, into their youthful minds such principles of moral conduct and initiate them into the principles and teachings of the Cause with such tactful and loving care as would enable them to become 'true sons of God' and develop into loyal and intelligent citizens of His Kingdom. This is the high purpose which Bahá'u'lláh Himself has clearly defined as the chief goal of every education.[1]

Donald Pope Some form of discipline is always needed. The greatest despair for a spiritual child ought to be disappointing his parents, not displeasing them but disappointing them. Most children are so caught up in today's self-centred culture that they could not care less what anyone thinks, let alone their parents. For them, removal of privileges or a series of rewards and punishments is called for. Taking what a child values and using it as an incentive is the best course. Removal of something that a child values, such as privileges, also works. Acknowledgement and praise (or other rewards) for doing the right thing is effective.

Katayun Golshani We did all of the above. If the behaviour was insignificant and was not part of a pattern, then I would ignore it. I'd consider this as something to be looked into for possible causes. I would look at it with compassion and see how it can be helped. The best attitude at all times is one of, 'Let me see how I can help my child not to repeat this.' Only make something an issue when you have to.

I've seen parents embarrass their children by demanding that the child say 'thank you'. You don't need to embarrass the child. If the child feels okay about it, it's fine. Everything should be done in a spirit of love. It's very important that the children feel loved rather than embarrassed. If the child might be embarrassed, the parent should save the discussion for later in private. You can give him a secret signal to remind him.

If the punishment is a matter of the child's safety, I would be very abrupt with the punishment. If the child runs across the street, for example, I would be very abrupt.

If I am angry at the child, perhaps that is not a good moment to administer discipline. I would be very reserved about the kind of reaction I would give to my child. Times of anger are not my best moments as a parent because I'm hijacked by my own emotions. A parent needs to really be able to get into her own head when correcting a child and to not to be locked in by her own emotions. The parent needs to be able to really stand back and put the emotion into perspective. The well-being and long-term welfare

THE PRINCIPLE OF OBEDIENCE

of the child needs to always be kept in mind before doing anything about discipline. That should be the rule of thumb. Never act in any direction towards your child when you're so hijacked by your own emotions – especially when you feel things such as anger or disappointment or when you're taking things personally such as, 'This child has disrespected me'. You're not going to be doing something that you'll be happy about later. Wait. Take a break. The parent can tell the child, 'I feel really upset and angry. I'm going to take a time-out myself because if I act right now, I'm going to say or do something that I won't like. I'm going to sit down, say a prayer and take a time-out. We can talk about it later.' You then don't lash out and get out of control with your emotions. You wait and you act based on your higher, spiritual self, not just your emotional, temporary self.

Julie Young Privileges were withdrawn. Also, they were given time-outs. This was called 'think-about' time. The length depended on their age, usually about one minute per year (for example, at the age of five, it was a five-minute time-out). As they got a little older, it could be for the entire afternoon. Time-outs were given anywhere and immediately – in the car or any public place. If we were in the car, we would pull the car over to the side. Once they were teenagers, privileges were withdrawn. For example, they were not allowed the use of the car. It had to be something that really mattered to them, otherwise the punishment was meaningless.

Harriet Douglas Punishments were almost never called for. Privileges were only withdrawn if the actions seemed particularly dangerous or disruptive and other means had failed to bring about an understanding of the need for change. Sometimes we did prefer to ignore the bad behaviour if we could begin to define 'bad' behaviour as a need for loving attention or a response to some sort of underlying pain or fear. It could help us see how to remedy the situation with minimal damage and estrangement. As soon as you notice that you are *reacting* rather than acting with love and concern, as 'Abdu'l-Bahá would act, you have lost the main objective and need to do whatever it takes to return to love. You should then give yourself a time-out until you're re-centred.

Andrew Adams The type of punishment depends on the age of the child. Consult about the crime first (in private). Make sure the child knows what he did wrong. Make sure the child knows that you know what he did wrong. Overlook mistakes. Punish intentional wrongdoing. Remove the child from the social situation. Spend time with the child yourself. For older children, removing privileges can work but if overused will produce frustration and resentment. The best means of correcting a child's behaviour is to spend time with the child following the poor choice of behaviour. Patiently guide the child.

Margerie Gibson That would depend upon *why* I think she is misbehaving. If it is a matter of immaturity, I might have a short time-out and then discuss better and more effective ways to communicate her needs.

If she is trying to engage me in a power struggle, which shows up as stubbornness and belligerence, I back off and try to provide choices for her to act upon, thus engaging her in forward motion towards a goal, rather than a tussle over who's in control.

If the behaviour stems from sheer meanness, then I withdraw privileges like play dates or treats like hot cocoa (a regular thing).

If the behaviour is from being overtired, I overlook really minor things; but with more annoying actions, I try to calmly discuss how she can take a moment to figure out what the problem is, what solutions she might desire and come up with more effective ways to gain cooperation from us.

Sometimes I yell at her in a completely unproductive way that ends up leading to yet another discussion on how ineffective mommy's method of communication was.

Melissa Taheri We rarely ignored bad behaviour and always talked about it later so that they knew what they had done wrong and what to do in the future. Privileges were denied and time-outs were used. Warnings were given but after that action was taken. If they misbehaved at a store, we left. That happened only a few times. When the boys were young we went to the grocery store as a family. If there was bad behaviour, one of us would take that child out to the car and wait.

Grace Simpson When she was small I would send her to her room. When she got older, I took away the thing she loved the most – her stereo. That really worked!

Bernice McKenzie My husband and I were both brought up by parents who beat us. In 1977 the Hand of the Cause of God Mr Faizi came to New Zealand for an international conference and spoke to the friends about bringing up children and about the importance of not hitting children. From that time on, we did not hit the children. We told the children (they would have been eight and nine) that we would not hit them again and they had the responsibility not to get us to the point where we would want to hit them. We would send them to their room, have them do extra chores and sometimes not let them go someplace they had planned to go.

What is your opinion on spanking (smacking) – that is, a mild swat on the hand or a swat on the bottom?

Whensoever a mother seeth that her child hath done well, let her praise and applaud him and cheer his heart; and if the slightest undesirable trait should manifest itself, let her counsel the child and punish him, and use means based on reason, even a slight verbal chastisement should this be necessary. It is not, however, permissible to strike a child, or vilify him, for the child's character will be totally perverted if he be subjected to blows or verbal abuse.[2]

As to your question about the use of physical punishment in child training, although there is a Tablet of the Master which considers beating as not permissible, this does not necessarily include every form of corporal punishment. In order to have a full grasp of the Master's attitude towards punishment, one has to study all His Tablets in this respect. For the time being no hard and fast rule can be laid down, and parents must use their own wise discretion in these matters until the time is ripe for the principles of Bahá'í education of children to be more clearly elucidated and applied.[3]

Donald Pope Spanking or other forms of physical punishment are the least effective forms of discipline, particularly if used often. Physical punishment, if severe enough, may get a child to stop doing something but will never get him to do the right thing. Acknowledgement and praise (or other rewards) for doing the right thing is much more effective. Hitting a child, when done rarely, to emphasize a point or to show frustration, is something every parent does and it often gets the point across. Spanking as a common parenting practice builds resentment, anger and rebellion. Use encouragement: it is far more effective.

Donna Smith I spanked. I don't think I would now. But children can sometimes drive you to distraction. I didn't spank a lot but I did spank when I reached the end of my rope. They knew I meant it. I have talked with them as adults about this. They tell me they never resented it and knew they deserved it. But just the same, I would only advise spanking as the very last resort. Some children are much easier than others to raise.

Margerie Gibson A child is too old to be spanked from birth. Spanking teaches nothing but how to hit. It damages the child's spirit.

Michelle Sharpe We spanked in the past and in the early years. I would never advise it. It only works in the short term and nothing is really learned here. I feel that spanking teaches the child to resort to violence as a solution. I believe in speaking to the child and taking appropriate action on behaviour. Spanking develops anger in the child and creates a character flaw.

THE PRINCIPLE OF OBEDIENCE

Simon Scott We spanked on occasion and I have no problem with it. At some point in the future, someone can ask my daughters their opinion. I do not believe they will have any problem with the discipline meted to them, nor have they been physically or psychologically scarred.

Kevin Johnson Before I became a Bahá'í, I spanked – a mild swat. After I became a Bahá'í, I stopped. It's wrong. It's a weakness. It produces resentment. And it teaches the child to hit.

Bernice McKenzie I do not believe in spanking *except* if the child runs out in the middle of the road where a car could hit her. Then it would be a whack on the bottom.

Todd and Debbie McEwen Generally, smacking does not work well. If children are well disciplined when they are young, and understand the boundaries, there is no need to have such a severe punishment as spanking at all.

Julie Young We did not really spank. Occasionally, we would slap their hands if they were going somewhere dangerous, such as trying to touch the stove. Our rule of thumb was that we would hit on the bottom if they did something dangerous (running out into the street, for example) but we rarely had to do this.

John and Barbara Hartley Spanking should only take place when the child puts himself in danger – for example, crossing the road without looking. Otherwise, I don't feel a child should be spanked. A talk is much more effective.

Edyth Lewis For a young child this may be appropriate in certain circumstances but needs to be used very sparingly and not become the first line of action. Once you can reason with a child it should not be necessary at all.

What did you do about children answering back and always demanding the last word?

The children must be carefully trained to be most courteous and well-behaved.[4]

The Guardian, in his remarks to . . . about parents' and children's, wives' and husbands' relations in America, meant that there is a tendency in that country for children to be too independent of the wishes of their parents and lacking in the respect due to them . . .[5]

Donna Smith We had one child like this. That is why I went grey young! But seriously, with some children you need to be very gentle because they bruise easily and you must be sensitive to them. Others are like a Mack truck – they only understand a cement wall. When this child would talk back to us, we added penalties (after warning) and we stuck with those penalties. We would explain again and again that when two people argue both are wrong and we are the parents and that is that. He hated it at the time but it was necessary. He is still strong but mature and sensitive and will probably rule the world someday (again just kidding!) but his strength is now under his mature self. Nevertheless, training a child like this is like training a stallion and is a little different from training a cute puppy.

Children have no right to answer back. Parents parent the children, not the other way around.

Donald Pope Tell them that when they speak to you respectfully then you will listen. If they choose to argue, just walk away. You do not need your child to agree with you. God placed you in charge. You do not need your child's consent. You have no need to argue. You cannot win without anger and resentment being the result. When your child speaks with respect, stop what you are doing and listen. Consider what is said and then respond with respect.

Andrew Adams Talking back is not allowed. It violates the basic parent–child relationship. The parent is boss. The child is not.

THE PRINCIPLE OF OBEDIENCE

Julie Young When they were younger, this was easy. It was simply unacceptable. They were given punishments, usually in the form of a time-out. As they got older, they learned to have more logical explanations. We would listen and let them say what they needed to say. We would then ask them if they were finished. We would repeat what they had said and made sure that we understood their point. In the end, we had the final word and would tell them, 'That's all we're going to talk about today. Maybe we'll continue tomorrow.'

Katayun Golshani As a parent, we need to remember as much as we can that the behaviour of a child is not about us and it's not about *that particular moment*. As parents, we need to look at patterns of behaviour rather than looking at an incident by itself.

Obviously, if it is the first time a child answers back and is disrespectful, rather than focusing on the negative, the parent should gently and lovingly remind them about the way they'd like the child to respond, thereby giving them a positive model. You gently and lovingly teach them to say, 'Yes, Mommy' or 'No thank you, Mommy' rather than 'Shut your mouth' or some other rude response.

Always be aware of the model you are showing as you are trying to teach and correct your children. Parents need to make sure that the child knows and understands the importance of respect but we also need to give them respect. If the relationship between child and parent is respectful, there is little chance that a child will answer back.

Parents need to be very clear when they make a request or when they set a boundary. Is it something which is optional and negotiable to the child or is it something that is absolute and non-negotiable? If it is negotiable, let him know. Make it clear to the child what is negotiable and what is not. If it is non-negotiable, the parents' tone of voice and no-nonsense approach has to be there and it has to be firm.

Making empty threats and saying things that you don't really mean sets the parents up for this kind of talking back from their children.

Giving in after lots of pleading and insisting is also a set-up for disaster. If the parents give in after one minute, I can assure you that the next time the child will go on for five minutes and he won't give up. When they give in after five minutes, the next time it will be forever. It is the parents who set the pattern and the style. You can tell the child that this issue is open for consultation and that this other issue is not. Don't allow the child to change something that you really don't want to change. Don't be intimidated. Don't try to win the approval of your child.

As you go, introduce the Bahá'í principle to the child. Let them know why you made the decision you made. They should become fully aware that there is no negotiation or compromise with regard to Bahá'í principles. Attending Feast, for example, is non-negotiable. But the parents need to make sure that Feast is pleasant and enjoyable for the child. Or if the child wants to watch a programme on TV that you consider to be inappropriate, that is simply non-negotiable, no matter how much the child presses you. You can humour him, you talk to him, you tell him, 'Wow, you'll really make a good lawyer! But this is one of those areas that won't be changing at all because this is a principle.'

It's essential to have a good relationship with the child to be able to get through these rough spots. A good relationship is indispensable.

Parents need to be wise and to be very careful about the battles they choose. Don't make *every* single thing a reason for having a battle. This will damage the relationship. The child will be constantly fighting you just for the fight. The relationship will become a subject of constant struggle.

Tom and Andrea Edwards We tried to 'nip it in the bud'.

Michelle Sharpe Sometimes we argued with them, which, looking back now, was not the right thing to do. Sometimes we asked them how they were feeling and they would go from anger to tears. We found the more we asked them how they were feeling, the more we made headway.

THE PRINCIPLE OF OBEDIENCE

Edyth Lewis Our children tended not to answer back if they saw reasoning behind our demands. The occasions when there was trouble was usually when we did not have the time to explain properly to them why we would not allow an action on their part or if they saw our argument as weak. With consultation we were able to resolve most issues and they would accept our decisions. Occasionally we would modify our demands having listened to what they had to say.

Joe and Wilma Thompson No way! We respected them and they respected us. And for good reason, not just because we were the parents! If we saw them showing an attitude, it would be discussed. For some time, we had a problem with this with one of our daughters. Reflection on the writings and time resolved this.

Phoebe Untekar I didn't handle that very well. I often let myself get hooked into a battle of wits.

Lucy Matthews Mostly I laughed! But then I laughed at most things! Then I'd say, 'But honey, that sounds so immature! Straighten up.' When she was about seven and said, 'I hate you!' I said, 'I know you do, honey. It's all right. I know you're mad.' I was not a very good disciplinarian, I'm afraid. Things amused me. Sometimes I felt that I shouldn't laugh and that I should be taking her more seriously. If she came to me with a problem, I wouldn't laugh. That was something else.

When and how did you explain to your child some of the laws of the Faith that would apply to them when they reached the age of 15, for example obligatory prayer, fasting and Ḥuqúqu'lláh?

Irene Dominguez We really began explaining the laws to them when they were nine or ten. Of course, they always saw us fasting and saying the obligatory prayer. They were also taught about these at children's and junior youth classes.

Paul Oliver Obligatory prayer and fasting were just part of the family conversation. The children saw us doing these things. We could have done a better job with Ḥuqúqu'lláh, although we all attended conferences about it and learned about it together.

Bernice McKenzie My eldest would come into my bedroom when I said my long obligatory prayer and watch me. She was about six at the time. My husband and I kept the fast and the children observed that process. When they wanted to keep the fast, we said they could try but Bahá'u'lláh said they didn't need to keep the fast until they were 15. So when they tried to fast as children, they usually made it all the way to morning tea! We didn't have Ḥuqúqu'lláh at the time but they were very aware of the importance of sacrifice with regard to the fund.

Lucy Matthews As I grew up, I was aware of these things since my parents were fasting. They told me that I couldn't fast since I wasn't old enough. All these things were a natural part of growing up. I knew about them. We didn't have Ḥuqúqu'lláh but we had the Bahá'í funds. With our daughter, we talked about these things at home as well as in summer schools. I loved the junior youth sessions! They would ask them, 'Who has memorized the long obligatory prayer?' Some hands would go up. They would then tell them, 'Well, you better start memorizing it soon.'

Linda Paulson Prayer has always been part of our daily lives. The children saw their parents say the long obligatory prayer every day. They usually came into the room when we were praying and joined us. I think if you want your children to say the obligatory prayer every day, they have to see you do it. Therefore, the children's father and I started saying our prayers in the living room. We'd turn off the TV if it was on, explain we were going to say our prayers and the kids would see how it was done and hear it every day. It was a normal part of their day. We also had family prayer time at the end of the day when they would say a prayer or two.

The children usually received presents for Ayyám-i-Há. Then

THE PRINCIPLE OF OBEDIENCE

they'd see their parents fast each year and ask about it. When they asked, we'd explain it to them in ways they could understand. As for Ḥuqúqu'lláh, we've discussed it at various times and taken them to the classes that have been offered in recent years.

Phoebe Untekar We started talking about these things as soon as they were old enough to understand, often relating them to laws of nature. We had discussions about our own experiences with those laws.

Joe and Wilma Thompson They saw us do this and expected it when they became Bahá'ís. Example was the best teacher, although we were not perfect!

Beth Bishop They learned about fasting from seeing me fast. I told them about obligatory prayer but they also learned about this in Bahá'í school. I used to encourage them to contribute to the fund by having a pot in the bedroom that they could put money in, which was then given in at the Feast.

Melissa Taheri: When they were 12 or 13 we began talking informally about the laws. They have seen us trying to live the laws all their lives, so most were not new. As they've got older we've also explained that the laws are why our family does certain things the way it does. I think most of the laws had been absorbed by the time they were 15, as a part of life.

3
Teaching Your Child the Principle of Trustworthiness and Integrity

Small children often can't distinguish fact from fiction and are great at making up fantasies or stories when talking to others. By adult standards, this is sometimes considered to be lying. Did you correct your child when this occurred or did you consider this to be a normal part of childhood?

> Truthfulness is the foundation of all the virtues of the world of humanity. Without truthfulness, progress and success in all of the worlds of God are impossible for a soul. When this holy attribute is established in man, all the divine qualities will also become realized.[1]

Donald Pope Lying is a normal part of growing up. The logic of young children is such that it isn't really a lie until you admit it. The parent has to be an agent for the truth. If children tell a story, you might say, 'What a great story. Now tell me what actually happened.' If you know something to be true and a child says something else, you might say, 'I am not fooled. Here is the truth and here is what is going to happen as a result.'

As a child gets older, you should have a discussion that lets the child know that truth is the foundation of trust. Every child wants her parent to trust her. If they always tell the truth then the trust will come easily.

THE PRINCIPLE OF TRUSTWORTHINESS AND INTEGRITY

Andrew Adams Ask yourself the question, 'What is the child's intention?' If the intention is pure, this is no problem. If the intention is to deceive, then stop it.

Katayun Golshani Lying becomes lying when there's intent to deceive. Young children don't yet have the cognitive ability to deceive or to be deliberate. When the child indulges in fantasies or stories, the parent can gently guide him. I want to emphasize that raising children is not about the moment. Raising children is about raising them with integrity and spiritual qualities, to learn the value of being truthful. If the child says that he's already washed his hands before a meal and you know that he has not, your response should be, 'I think you should wash your hands. You need to wash your hands.' As he gets older, you shouldn't let him get away with it or the child will learn that if he can trick and deceive his parents, he can deceive and trick others too.

Edyth Lewis If any of the children lied, then I made sure that they knew that I knew they were not telling the truth. Much depended on the severity of the lie and at what age they were and why they were lying. I always made sure that they knew that the liar would eventually be found out and that it would be better to tell the truth up front.

There were also occasions when I suspected that they were lying and gave them an opportunity to tell me the truth without getting into trouble or get into less trouble, for the misdemeanour that they were trying to cover up.

I also made sure that they were aware of the significance of the story of the boy who cried 'wolf'.

George and Mary Burke Learning to tell the truth begins at birth. Integrity and honesty are the most critical qualities a child can develop because Bahá'u'lláh says that without this quality no other qualities are possible. When a child is old enough to know right from wrong, they are then capable of telling the truth or not telling the truth. This occurs between the ages of two and five.

Joe and Wilma Thompson Honesty was probably *the* most important attribute stressed in their young lives. One of the only times we were physical with a daughter in punishment is when we thought that she had told an untruth! She says she always remembered that lesson although she had not been lying! The deafness and language were often barriers and it took much more time and patience to handle situations. *My* prayers were often for this!

Irene Dominguez We've always tried to make them tell the truth. We've encouraged them to tell the most exact way that things have occurred. But we have not punished them, although we've sometimes had to ask them the same thing twice. They learned to tell the truth from a very young age and this is key. We became more strict about this by the time they were five or six. We helped them with this, by encouraging them to as honest and accurate as possible.

Julie Young My children did not always tell the truth. When children are young, they often lie and this is very normal for me. They lie to protect themselves. We have to train and teach them that lying is not acceptable. We have to remind them that we know. For example, 'I know who knocked over the vase. Can you tell me who did? I'll give you one more chance to be honest.' Then praise them for their honesty. When they are little, sit them down and say that you saw them knock over the vase. You must model what you want to happen.

A different thing sets in when the children get older. They start to make judgements about how bad the consequences can be. I would always sit them down and tell them to remember that even if I don't personally know what the truth is, God knows and let's pray that God will give us the strength to be truthful. They were always taught to pray when they did something wrong.

THE PRINCIPLE OF TRUSTWORTHINESS AND INTEGRITY

What would you do about chronic, persistent lying?

The individual must be educated to such a high degree that he would rather have his throat cut than tell a lie, and would think it easier to be slashed with a sword or pierced with a spear than to utter calumny or be carried away by wrath.[2]

Donald Pope Persistent lying is not normal. The most important thing is for the parent to let the child know that the parent knows the difference between a lie and the truth and that the parent is not being fooled. Too often, parents want the child to admit that she is lying. This then sets up a power struggle. Persistent lying is often a control battle.

Andrew Adams Ask yourself the question, 'What is the child's intention?' If the intention is to deceive, then it must be stopped.

Katayun Golshani It depends on the age of the child. Lying itself is a symptom. We, as the parents, have to ask why this child is lying and what has happened that has led it to become chronic. What has reinforced this behaviour? Is the child afraid to talk to the parent? With older children, whenever there's chronic lying, the issue of drugs and alcohol needs to be looked at. You need to be systematic when looking into the relationship between the parent and the child, as well as the dynamic of the household. Why is this child not telling the truth? What are the consequences of telling the truth? Getting help from a competent counsellor would be very good.

Marva Ross Lying was punished.

Edyth Lewis This became a bit of a problem when one of our sons was a teenager. We tried to decide when we thought he was lying and when he was not and what his motives were for lying but sometimes it was impossible to tell whether what he was telling us was true or not. He seemed to give this up after a while. With a persistent liar the only thing you can do is to challenge everything he says, even when you know something is true. He quickly realizes that he needs to revise his behaviour.

Donna Smith There must be a source. The word 'chronic' means just that. I would have nipped it in the bud. I would not tolerate it at all. It would have been clear. By the time it is chronic, it means that they have somehow been getting away with it for a long time.

Linda Bandari I did not have any big problem with my children chronically lying. I always told them that I would be much more understanding if they told me the truth. Sometimes it took a while but normally they would come and tell me the truth or tell on one another.

Michelle Sharpe Thank God lying was never a problem. Many miscommunications were perceived to be lying. However, when we got to the bottom, we got to the truth. Our children were very conscious of telling the truth. They also quickly noticed adults or children who lied.

John and Barbara Hartley We didn't have that problem. For the occasional lie, we would point out that we knew what they were saying was untrue and if they wanted us to believe them, they had better start telling the truth.

What would you do if you found out that your child cheated on a test?

John and Barbara Hartley We would make him tell the teacher and allow whatever consequences the teacher gave.

Tanya Charles I would be so concerned to find out my child had cheated on a test. Unfortunately, this is common even among 'good' students and lots of kids don't even see this as a problem if

THE PRINCIPLE OF TRUSTWORTHINESS AND INTEGRITY

they don't get caught. So the first thing is that you should be glad that your child got caught! This sounds terrible but, really, this allows for intervention. If he hadn't got caught, this never would have happened. So think positive.

For this issue I would definitely want to consult with the school-teacher and/or counsellor. This is one topic I don't have personal experience with and they will have lots of experience with it. However, just because they are the 'experts,' don't think you have to accept everything they say. You know your child better than they do. I would be sure to support the school in whatever its consequences were.

Also, be sure to speak with your child! Actually, what I mean to say is, be sure to listen to your child. Ask something open like, 'Tell me about this.' Then listen. Is she under pressure to succeed? Is he not understanding the material? Was she so busy, she didn't have time to study? Was he under peer pressure to cheat? By listening you can learn about the root cause for the cheating and can work to change that. I recommend that this listening time not be given to discussion by you if you are upset. Give yourself a chance to calm down and consider things before working with your child to correct things.

Remember, too, the importance of an apology. I would ask my child to consider writing an apology to the teacher involved. We encourage our kids to try to do two steps to correct mistakes: fix it as best you can and apologize. Because I think it's important that an apology be sincere, I would not force the child to write it. Perhaps I would write one if he didn't and let the teacher know how glad I was that this had been brought to my attention so that my child and I could work to rectify things.

Grace Simpson I would take her into class and have her apologize to the teacher. I would then see what the writings say about that.

Linda Bandari If my child cheated on a test I would try to find out why it happened and see if there was a deeper problem that was bothering him that may have been part of it. I would let my child know that cheating was not okay and if it happened again there would be consequences – the loss of privileges. I would also have my child talk to the teacher and/or school officials and apologize.

George and Mary Burke Children should receive appropriate consequences for cheating: zero on the test; academic probation and so on. Parents need to support honesty wholeheartedly.

Simon Scott If we found out, I would assume that the teacher already had knowledge of the incident and implemented some form of punishment. I would support this, discuss cheating as a moral/ethical flaw and possibly apply some form of additional punishment. Bahá'ís are given the twin pillars of 'reward and retribution'. That should apply for all society.

Irene Dominguez Talk to the child calmly. Make him see that it was wrong. Then ask why he did it, understand how he feels about it. Show him that cheating is lying. Talk about the importance of truthfulness.

From what age did you allow your child to go out without parental supervision?

Joe and Wilma Thompson Both girls were with peers that we had met – for skating, sports and movies – from the time they were 12 and 14. We would always ask where, with whom and for how long, so there would be an understanding of the activity. They were trusted early and knew this. They would often say they felt 'noble' ('Noble have I created thee . . .'[3]) and would attempt to conduct themselves like queens! They knew they could call us to come and get them if there were any problems or surprises that made them uncomfortable. We were fortunate in that they were both very mature for their ages. Perhaps having dealt with the deafness issue made them so. I am not sure.

THE PRINCIPLE OF TRUSTWORTHINESS AND INTEGRITY

Irene Dominguez From the time they were 15. But this always depended on the activity. We didn't allow them to go simply to hang out or fool around. They were allowed to attend parties at the homes of friends from the time they were 17. We always encouraged them to go in groups, not alone.

Richard and Theresa Baker If they were with Bahá'í friends, from about 12 or 13. With their school friends, they would also go out in a group at about the same age but we were less relaxed about it.

Edyth Lewis When we lived in the islands we lived in a safe environment and the children were allowed to roam freely from the age of about four. My daughter used to go stomping over the hill to see her friends. I would call the mother and check that it was okay. I could see her from the window for half her journey and her friends' mother could see her coming the rest of the way.

When they grew older and we moved, I always encouraged them to bring their friends back home. This meant that I knew what they were up to and what company they were keeping even if it did turn our home into a youth club at times.

Todd and Debbie McEwen This depended on the group they wanted to go out with, where they wanted to go and how we felt they would cope with problems. Local trips with a group of friends (within walking distance) was from around the age of 12. Trips that were further afield, involving public transport, were from around the age of 14.

Farzaneh Knight We live on a small island. Our children virtually grew up with their peer group since they were school age. They attended a small private school where we know most of the parents and their classmates. We have been lucky to be able to have a high level of trust in their peers. This, coupled with our clear perception that both girls had thoroughly internalized their Bahá'í values (they would even take their prayer books with them for overnight stays) allowed us always to trust them. Ironically, because of this, they had great freedom and no curfews and were highly responsible. They never abused that freedom. I have often told them, 'I will not be with you all the time to watch over you but 'Abdu'l-Bahá *is*. If you do something that you are happy to have 'Abdu'l-Bahá know about, then go for it. Otherwise, don't do it.'

Melissa Taheri The boys went to movies with friends probably starting at the age of 12 or 13. They would be dropped off at the beginning of the movie and picked up at the end. Movies were screened and they weren't allowed to see very many. They were 16 or so before going out for an evening with a friend. I knew the friend, where they were going, what they would be doing and when they would be back.

How do you feel about checking on your child from time to time? That is, checking their rooms, diaries, phone calls, etc.

Joe and Wilma Thompson We never did this. We didn't feel any real need to do so. I was their mother first and then their friend. They can only have one mother but many friends. In my opinion, mothers often confuse the two and it leads to confusion in the child's mind. At different times, both girls have said how they felt they could trust me totally. What a wonderful thing to hear! I may not have agreed but did not try to judge them. We would often ask them, 'What would you do in this situation?' to get them to think of situations before they occurred.

Julie Young We never felt that we needed to do that. We felt that we were on top of things, especially since we were always very actively involved in their lives. We did not feel that it was necessary to 'check' on them. We were so involved that we never even missed a single athletic event that they were at. They went with us and came home with us.

THE PRINCIPLE OF TRUSTWORTHINESS AND INTEGRITY

Tom and Andrea Edwards If I was afraid that the child was involved in something serious, I might check. Otherwise, I think the principle of trustworthiness prevails. That is, them trusting us not to invade their privacy secretly.

Donna Smith I never 'checked' their rooms but if I found anything which was questionable accidentally while tidying and cleaning up (and I did), they heard about it. We had a consultation and it was brought out into the open and discussed. I never looked at their diaries. I have three sons and boys generally don't keep diaries. But I hope that I wouldn't violate that trust. I never listened to their phone calls but I did restrict the length of time they were on the phone. Again, they hated that but I felt that they shouldn't constantly tie up the phone. If my children wanted their own phone, they would have to pay for it. I know I may sound draconian to some!

George and Mary Burke As children mature, they deserve measured doses of responsibility and privacy. If a parent feels compelled to 'check' or 'snoop' the personal belongings of their children, this is a symptom of lost trust that has accumulated over time. Suspicion needs to be addressed openly and honestly, not secretly.

Edyth Lewis If you have brought up your children properly then there should be some trust that would go both ways by the time they are teenagers. They were told that their rooms were their own areas. I did not even go in to clean. That was for them to do.

Paul Oliver If there is a reason to be suspicious at all, it is appropriate. A parent is responsible before God for the training and education of his children.

Todd and Debbie McEwen We do not check on personal papers, diaries or phone calls. We would only check their rooms to make sure that they had tidied them up when asked.

Richard and Theresa Baker As a matter of course (and tidiness) I would check their rooms quite regularly. I considered it a part of parenting.

Lucy Matthews I know of cases where, thank goodness, the parents did find out about things. Our daughter didn't keep a diary. The telephone was where everyone could hear her. Unfortunately, I think that parents now need to check on their children periodically. We live in a sick society.

Simon Scott I approve and have done it. They have complete personal privacy but actions require me to be vigilant. Thus far, we have had no problems along this line.

Did you allow your children to lock their doors? What if they said, 'It's MY room!'

Andrew Adams Our kids know that they are kids living in our (their parents') home. Everything in the house belongs to us, whether it is in the room that they sleep in or not. There are no secrets. They are not allowed to keep secrets from us; we do not keep secrets from them. We are a family. We live together. Each individual has a right to personal privacy, in the bathroom or for changing clothes. Each has a right to personal space, for prayer or study. Neither child owns his room, clothes, toys or any other items in the home, even if given to them by someone else. The child's money is my money. I determine what is best for the child. In order to do that, I need to have total control of the child's environment.

Donna Smith Our children were allowed to lock their doors. I did knock before entering their rooms. When they said, 'It's *my* room and I'll do what I want!' my response was to consult with them about rights and responsibilities. After all it's my fridge, my food, my car and so on.

THE PRINCIPLE OF TRUSTWORTHINESS AND INTEGRITY

Katayun Golshani We did not have locks on any of our doors. When children are very small and they don't know about knocking, you can lock your own doors so that they don't interrupt or disturb your privacy. As far as knocking on doors, I think it's always nice for parents to model what they expect their children to do. You don't want anyone coming to your room without knocking. Parents should also apologize to their children when they do something wrong. They need to model what they want their children to do. Just because you're the adult, does not mean that these rules should be any different.

I made the rule, and I like the rule, that when children, particularly youth, bring their friends over, their bedroom door needs to be open unless there is a very good, legitimate reason for it to be closed. Once you set that rule then there are certain expected behaviours and they know the bedroom is not the place to be engaged in any inappropriate behaviour.

The truth is that it all comes to the issue of your relationship with the child. But the most important thing is how their relationship is with Bahá'u'lláh. If they have a good, solid, loving, firm relationship with Bahá'u'lláh, you really are going to be able to be a lot more relaxed about some of these rules and regulations. As they get older, they're going to be even more concerned about protecting themselves. So you watch from a distance to make sure that they're in an environment that supports that relationship with Bahá'u'lláh but you're not the one that's going to be there every moment controlling every little thing.

Basically the parent's role is one of a lessening of control as the child gets older and putting into place all those fundamental relationship bases – the child's relationship with God has to come first, the child's relationship with his parents and the child's relationship with his own self. These three have to be loving and solid. As the child grows, you lessen the control and offer the child more room and more choices.

Julie Young Generally, I knocked on their doors before entering but they never had locks on their doors. After all, their rooms were our rooms (the parents' rooms, that is). The parents pay the rent or own the house.

Melissa Taheri One of our sons does lock his door in the evenings when he's studying but he does open it when I knock. I have always tried to knock before entering, even when the door is open.

Linda Bandari My children sometimes locked their bedroom door when they were mad at each other and did not want the other one to come into his room. They kept their doors open much of the time. I never felt that I had to knock before entering their rooms but when the door was closed I called out their name and waited for a response before entering. They knew that it was their room but my house and my rules prevailed as long as they lived there. Fortunately I had a good relationship with my kids and we were able to talk through most problems that arose.

Richard and Theresa Baker Our son wasn't interested in locking his room. Our daughter liked to have her privacy (usually from her elder brother), so she asked for a lock to be put on her room and we complied with her request. As a matter of courtesy, we would knock on the door, if it was closed, before entering.

Nina Sadaghiyan As far as I remember, they locked their doors to keep the sibling out. It is a good habit to knock on the door before entering. It teaches respect and manners.

Donald Pope Our children did not have locks on their doors but we did knock before entering. It is their room but you provide it. The same rules apply as they apply throughout the household. As long as you provide the room, you are responsible for what happens in it.

THE PRINCIPLE OF TRUSTWORTHINESS AND INTEGRITY

What are your rules on phone calls?

Linda Bandari The phone limit was ten minutes as my husband often had business calls coming in. It was usually my daughter who talked most on the phone, and it was her brother who normally let me know on the second when her ten minutes was up. Normally the limit was three phone calls a night, depending on the situation. My daughter would often talk in her room with her door closed, mainly so her brother wouldn't bother her. I normally knew who she was talking to. There was a big group of Bahá'í kids that hung out together and were almost inseparable. My daughter also had three very close school girlfriends who did a lot together and still keep in contact. My son did not have much interest in spending time on the telephone. He spent most of his time on the computer.

Richard and Theresa Baker They were free to use the phone when they wished but we used to point out to them the high cost of phone calls. When they began to earn their pocket money, we would ask for some reimbursement for their phone calls.

Simon Scott They are allowed phone calls and privacy when doing so. We have had to force the issue on when calls are not allowed, even requiring me to pick up another line and tell them that it is too late and to get off the phone.

Bernice McKenzie I always felt that being a teenager meant you would have a telephone glued to your ear for about four or five years. If my kids were on the phone, it meant that nobody could bother me! Nowadays, it's easier for kids, because we have call waiting and cell phones. I think teenagers love to talk and there is no harm in them being on the phone.

Grace Simpson When she was in elementary school, she was allowed only ten minutes on the phone per individual that she called. When she started high school, we got call waiting. She was allowed to have privacy.

Michelle Sharpe We have insisted that the phone calls be kept to a minimum. At homework times, we encourage the calls to be homework-related. The online chats were becoming an issue. We found we had to set strict guidelines. We need to know who they are chatting with and to be able to stand right beside them when they are chatting, without necessarily being nosey. We discourage closed doors. I must say we are strict in these areas.

Tom and Andrea Edwards Phone calls were allowed after homework. The time on the phone was limited. They were allowed privacy.

Lucy Matthews As our daughter got older, I got her a long line/extension cord. She was allowed to go to her room and close the door while on the phone. We always emphasized to her that we respected and trusted her. We told her that if she didn't deserve the trust, we would eventually find out and then we wouldn't trust her. We talked about trustworthiness. I told her that if she was not trustworthy, it would backfire. She would lose in the end. We put it on a spiritual and practical basis.

Nina Sadaghiyan We had one phone in our home. We did not allow late night phone calls.

Farzaneh Knight Yes, they were entitled to full privacy. Since we knew who they were talking to, we did not feel uncomfortable with this. As far as time constraints, this depended on whether we felt it was excessive given the situation and if they had homework or chores. We set limits.

Donna Smith They were allowed 15 minutes on the phone. I set the buzzer. They hated it. They were allowed full privacy while on the phone.

4

Helping Your Child Understand the Principles of Chastity and Moderation

At what age did you talk to your child about sex and how did you introduce it?

Lucy Matthews My mother got me a booklet. She showed me pictures and talked about it. We then watched the kittens being born. I was about seven years old. She told me about reproduction and the importance of marriage. She talked about the difference between humans and cats and why we need both parents. She said that we grow more slowly and we are spiritual beings.

Margerie Gibson Gradually, starting from about age four or five, as natural curiosity sparked questions. I started out referring to 'sex' as 'special snuggles' between mommies and daddies, then at some point we saw the TV show *Miracle of Life* that filmed a foetus in the womb at the different stages of development. There's a book of it too, with many of the same pictures.

After the age of eight, we gradually introduced discussions about the spiritual connection that is created when men and women engage in 'special snuggles', along with an introduction to the word 'sex' as applied to the act, as well as to the gender.

Unfortunately, in 'modern' America, these discussions must come much sooner than they did for earlier generations. Young children are bombarded with sexual images from all sides. We don't even have television any more because I felt like I was losing the battle too many days with the media's obsession with sex. We just had to get it all out of our home.

Joe and Wilma Thompson As I remember we gave them the book *Where Did I Come From?* when they were about eight. They had the general knowledge and then were both taught about it in science/biology classes in college. Our society teaches facts. Facts are important but it is left up to the parents to teach morals. They had many conversations with other Bahá'ís during their teens. We also used Desmond Morris's book *Intimate Behaviour* to discuss the 12 levels of intimacy. Joe used this when talking with the Bahá'í youth about this issue. Another book that is an excellent resource for teens in this Bahá'í sub-culture is *How Far is Too Far?: Where to Draw the Line on Premarital Sex and Physical Intimacy* by Todd Lochner. This book makes boundaries very understandable.

Donna Smith Heck, they know more about sex than we do! They have all these boring classes on sex in such detail that we never dreamed of. School taught them the facts. What they weren't taught at school were the emotions and the spirit. That is what I talked about – the emotions of sex and the spirit of love. This could be difficult at times. It is hard to differentiate between the two when the hormones are raging.

Melissa Taheri I answered questions about sex whenever they came up. My five year old wanted to know where babies came from and I took the lead from his questions. When they were 11 or so and the subject was coming up at school, I also talked with them about sex and changes in their bodies. I had several pamphlets available from work and each knew where these were at home to look at. Most of our talks were spontaneous and they knew I would always try to answer anything.

THE PRINCIPLES OF CHASTITY AND MODERATION

What were your rules on dating?

Katayun Golshani In our household, we decided that dating was not a necessary state. The children were allowed and free to have friends of both sexes. If there was someone very special to one of them, he or she was encouraged to invite that person to come to our house. Our youngest daughter was invited to go to the prom by one of her school friends. I invited him over. We sat down and talked. I gave them both standards. I told them that I would like them to be going as two friends. They were each to pay for themselves. I also told them that I would like the Bahá'í laws of chastity to be observed. I told him that there was to be no drinking. I told them she was to be home by a certain time. I don't think parents should be shy about supervising or stating the values and standing by them. Encourage your children to share their values and standards of chastity with their friends.

Whenever I saw my children becoming more influenced by the behaviours and standards of their schoolmates than I wanted them to be, I would just take them to a Bahá'í school. It was so amazing. By being around other Bahá'í youth, their compass would be adjusted and they would rethink their attitudes. I found this to be very effective. Having good friends, going to places where there are noble youth, fortifying and readjusting the compass are all powerful.

Grace Simpson I told her she could not date until she was 16. Yes, I had to know the person she was going out with. I would take down his licence number, ask if he had insurance, told him that this was my daughter and that if anything happened to her, he would be responsible. I had to know where they were going, what time they would be back and if they were going to be any later than they said, they had to call. The curfew depended on what they were going to be doing.

Lucy Matthews When she was about 14, she was allowed to go to group parties but she couldn't date. When she was about 15, she was allowed to date. We consulted about dating and always said why she could or couldn't. We consulted as to what she was and wasn't permitted to do. When she started dating, she was only allowed to double-date at first (four of them). We weren't worried. We talked to her and asked her where she was going, who was going to be there, what time the event was to finish and so on. The boy had to come to the house and pick our daughter up. We had to talk to him. We told him the time that we expected her to be back home. We told him that we expected him to have her home by that time, and if not, she was the one who would be grounded. They had to call if there was a change in plans. Our daughter was allowed out on one weekend night but not both. Mostly, whatever she did, was in a group. As far as the rules went, I always told my daughter to tell her friends to blame us as her parents: 'I'll be in big trouble with my parents.' We told our daughter that we trusted her implicitly.

Donald Pope For a person who knows his spiritual worth and the importance of others, spiritually there are only two relationships possible – friendship and courtship. Dating as a rehearsal for marriage is too trivial and has no place. Friends can provide intimacy without sexuality. Courtship comes into play when you are exploring the character of another to make an eternal commitment. No one is allowed to date, only to be friends or to court another to discover his or her character. It all comes down to the child's understanding and the level of trust you have in him to make the best choices. Curfews are meant to keep the children safe and to confirm and earn your trust. Set them for that reason and change them as your trust grows. I should also add that I believe that people should make eternal exclusive commitments to another human being as early as possible.

John and Barbara Hartley The boys did not date early in their teens. They preferred to go to group events with their friends. It was something we didn't have to impose rules on as they decided on their own that going out with a group of friends was preferable to dating.

THE PRINCIPLES OF CHASTITY AND MODERATION

Linda Bandari Neither one of my children dated when they were in high school with the exception of going to the prom with a date. Actually my children preferred going out with a group of friends and thought it was more fun. They knew that I did not want them to get involved with anyone before they graduated from high school. When my daughter was a junior in high school there was a boy who was seriously interested in her and wanted to date her. We had a big discussion about it and my daughter decided on her own that she preferred not to get involved with anyone at her age. She wanted to be free to have fun and enjoy all of her friends with none of the pressures of dating. My children had a wonderful group of friends, both school friends and Bahá'í friends, that I liked very much and they had much fun together. My children and I had a very close relationship and still do, even though both of my children are married and have children of their own. My teenage nephew (17) who lives with us does not date but prefers just to have fun with his friends. He feels that having a girlfriend complicates life too much.

George and Mary Burke Our daughters are not allowed to date in the non-Bahá'í setting. They are allowed to go out in co-ed groups of friends, never in a 'love/commitment' relationship. We do encourage them to identify qualities and people they admire and we do encourage them to establish friendships with those individuals. So far, my daughters have only identified those qualities in Bahá'ís that they know, as both daughters have expressed a desire to marry a Bahá'í. There are many young Bahá'í men that they admire – they have never established an intimate relationship with any. They have both prescribed to the laws of chastity. Many times they feel very different from their school peers but have managed, through regular gatherings with their Bahá'í friends, at social and formal events, to find enjoyment in each other's company in a safe and non-threatening environment.

Donna Smith We were very strict until 15 – no dating – after that we were very aware and trusted them and also demanded that they be responsible because of these new rights. It went smoothly.

But I feel, looking back, that all the work has to be done in those first 15 years. By the time they were 15 they were perfectly clear and we trusted them to make appropriate decisions. It was just one more aspect of being a Baháʼí. Our sons didn't really do much dating until they were about 18. We had *Lights of Guidance* on the dining room table. Every night at supper one of the family members would read from it. We focused on sex, chastity and fidelity. We discussed it. We said normal may not be right. Right is what is in the writings. They were fine with that because that is how they were raised. We didn't have to know whom they were dating because by the time they were dating we knew the type of people they chose as friends. They would see for themselves very quickly and we kept our mouths shut. Also, they seemed to bring their friends of the opposite sex home. There was only one we wondered about – and our son caught on quicker than we did!

Julie Young No one was allowed to date as long as they were living in our house. All their prom dates were friends of the family. We talked about it beforehand. They had to go to their senior prom in a group. My understanding of the Baháʼí writings is that there is no place for dating and that the only time it should occur is in preparation for marriage. The best way to investigate a person's character is to serve with them.

What were your rules on curfews?

George and Mary Burke From the age of 16, their curfew is 11 p.m. on weekends, 9 p.m. on weekdays (but they are rarely out on weekdays).

Angela Brown Parents should most certainly impose curfews on children and youth regardless of their age. I think it would be irresponsible not to do so. After all, every child will push for more time and later curfews, as this is the nature of being young and greedy for life! So it isn't wrong to ask but parents are amiss, I

THE PRINCIPLES OF CHASTITY AND MODERATION

believe, if they don't consult on an appropriate time for the event in question. They should know exactly where the child is and with whom, and they should enforce the curfew. So many crimes and illicit activities happen after midnight, that it would be difficult to convince me that a young person will derive any benefit from being out after 11 or 12 at night.

The desire to socialize is at an all-time high in adolescence, so even if it means a lot of chaperoning and driving and hosting for a few years, this will help our children to enjoy their youth without the heartbreak of violence, drugs, sex and, in general, an unwholesome social life.

We have been to Naw-Rúz dances and parties as a family which have lasted well into the early morning hours. This and the special Holy Days seem to be the occasions for breaking the curfew!

Donna Smith Curfews were agreed on first. They were to be obeyed or we were to receive a phone call explaining why they could not be obeyed. We would then negotiate a new curfew for that evening if we felt it was warranted.

John and Barbara Hartley Curfews become a problem when the children enter their teens. We were very firm about curfews during the school week. Usually they could go to someone's home, stay for dinner, study or play and then be home by 9 p.m. On weekends they could stay out later. We never allowed them to wander. They were at a movie or at someone's home. They were not allowed to hang out anywhere, such as malls, streets, parks and so on. If they were unable to be home by curfew they were required to call. Regardless of where they went or with whom they went, we encouraged them to consider their personal safety. They were discouraged from getting into a vehicle if the driver had had anything to drink. Yes, they always had non-Bahá'í friends. We would always pick them up from parties if they felt unsafe.

Joe and Wilma Thompson We had curfew based on the activity. We did not have one set time.

Phoebe Untekar In high school it was 9 p.m. on school nights. It was later on weekends. Curfews also depended on their age.

Simon Scott I give them the time to be home and they comply. If they do not comply and there is not an excellent and reasonable reason for such, then we will impose an in-house penalty – 'grounding'. This hasn't really been a problem.

Katayun Golshani The issue of safety was key for me. I always had to know exactly where they were and who they were with. I needed to know the phone number of the place and the people who were there. I needed to know that they were not doing things that were outside of our rules and values. I needed to know how they were to get home. I always preferred getting them home myself. If not, I needed to know who was bringing them home. Whenever I took them somewhere, I would stop by, introduce myself to the parents and would be aware of what was going on. We didn't have any problems that were serious enough for me to take action.

If a pattern starts to develop where the person is not observing or respecting the curfew, the parents should not allow him or her to go anywhere for a week or so until they feel sure that the child will obey.

Richard and Theresa Baker We always used to ask them, before leaving, what time we should expect them home. If we thought it was going to be too late, we would say that we wanted them home earlier and my husband would make a point of picking them up at the hour we said.

How can we encourage our children to have higher moral standards than the society around us without making them feel isolated from classmates?

> He feels that the youth, in particular, must constantly and determinedly strive to exemplify a Bahá'í life. In the world around us we

THE PRINCIPLES OF CHASTITY AND MODERATION

see moral decay, promiscuity, indecency, vulgarity, bad manners – the Bahá'í young people must be the opposite of these things, and, by their chastity, their uprightness, their decency, their consideration and good manners, attract others, old and young, to the Faith. The world is tired of words; it wants example, and it is up to the Bahá'í youth to furnish it.[1]

Donna Smith They will be isolated. It is the price they have to pay for being Bahá'ís. But they will also be admired and have one or two close friends and the admiration of mature souls all around them. When you grow up as a Bahá'í, there is going to be a certain amount of isolation because of your standards. Therefore it may be a period of sacrifice in their lives. Will the child have lots of friends or a few close ones? This depends on so much. Some of our children need many friends, whereas others are content to be independent. Society is ill, so we can focus on bringing as much health into their lives as possible, such as trips with family and one friend per child and lots of Bahá'í events where they may meet and make important friends. This happened with our youngest son. He was basically ashamed of being a Bahá'í. Then when he was 12 or 13 he went to youth winter schools and made close friends. We also took him on pilgrimage. Now at 27, his closest friends are all these people, all strong, active and happy Bahá'ís. He is married to a dynamo in the Faith and his deepening process goes on! Parents cannot let up until they are 15. They must be vigilant. Each child is so different. Lots of consultation and prayer are needed. This is what got us through.

When they'd say, 'Well, all my friends are . . .' my response would be, 'So what?' I think that it's always wiser to speak in private with the child. Peer pressure goes on all your life. Why do they make such a big deal of it when kids are teens? Normal may not necessarily be healthy. And healthy is what the writings give us. We are always going dead against normal and what is around us in society. So be it.

Michelle Sharpe By showing them the example in the home. By telling them the truth about life. By talking about what happens to youth who engage in sex and drinking. By talking about the consequences. We always point out examples in the community. We talk about immodest dress, for example, as we are walking down the street; about teenage moms carrying their babies to school – a baby in one arm and a school bag in the other. These real-life examples make a huge impact on children. We explain to them why some girls or boys behave in certain ways. We tell them that the standards in all homes are different. We turn to the writings on living a modest and chaste life and on the wisdom of practising it.

Tom and Andrea Edwards We expect Bahá'í children to feel somewhat isolated from their classmates. That is part of becoming accustomed to hardship.

Tanya Charles I made an eight-sided stop sign with statements into a nine-pointed star with a list of nine questions (developed by a dear friend, Fairy Mae McKeirnan). These are questions that the family should ask: Is it safe? Is it healthy? Is it honest? Is it considerate? Is it legal? Can we afford it? Is there time? Are you ready for the responsibility? Is it in keeping with the principles of the Faith? Asking questions is significant in my opinion. This encourages discussion and consultation. I want to encourage discussion and sharing of information and ideas, particularly by our children! Let them explain why it is safe or affordable and so on. In the middle of the nine-pointed star I have written, 'Settle all things, both great and small, by consultation.'[2]

This nine-pointed star hangs in our kitchen and when our growing kids want new freedoms, we gather around the star and start consulting. This provides a standard, one which opens discussion and avoids seemingly arbitrary pronouncements from parents. We need to listen to our children. Let them express their ideas before we pronounce judgement. If we don't allow this, they will feel we don't know the facts and don't understand their perspective. With this tool, our youth will feel heard. One of the values of this tool is that it generates consultation and a thought-

THE PRINCIPLES OF CHASTITY AND MODERATION

ful presentation of ideas by the children and youth. They have to make the case, so to speak. This is training them in organizing and presenting ideas and in the consultative process. Also, this is practice in decision-making, providing them with a checklist for use in the future. What standards will they use for making choices when they are not under our supervision, whether at a friend's home or off at college? This is a nice standard to have practised.

Another benefit is that it can be less confrontational to be discussing the star together. It serves as a bit of a buffer. Rather than the parent saying 'no' straight away, the parent and child are discussing the issue with the buffer of an outside arbitrator, the star. This helps keep the lines of communication open and tempers from flaring.

Angela Brown I don't know whether it is entirely possible to inculcate the high standards of a Bahá'í in our children through daily life practices, examples and regular classes without setting them up for a little loneliness. I recall that a few years back, our son, who was then about nine or ten, seemed to be alone quite a bit, neither going out to play in the neighbourhood nor inviting others in. When I kept speaking with him about this matter, urging him to invite some of his friends over or to go out and play with them, he said, 'Mom, you don't understand what these kids are doing and what they are like!' When I tried to find out what behaviours or manners he was referring to, he felt that he would have to backbite in order to discuss the entire situation with me.

Now that he is older, our son seems better able to choose friends, though he still tends to feel that there must be limitations in his friendships. On the other hand, when my daughters were children and youth they tended to find several non-Bahá'í friends who accepted them as Bahá'ís and who were even willing to participate from time to time in Bahá'í events, inviting my daughters to some of their religious events occasionally.

Moral standards and issues should always be discussed, although our children have always expressed discomfort when we bring them up, especially regarding sex, drugs and relationships.

It seems that many young people outside of the Faith are left with little in the way of clear guidance, which creates many confusing moral situations for them. I have gone over passages in the *Kitáb-i-Aqdas* and in the Master's writings. It is clear what behaviours are not allowed and – as much as possible – why. I think such guidance and discussion is best before the temptations to hold hands, to kiss, to touch inappropriately, to smoke cigarettes and marijuana or to drink alcohol present themselves. While these may be discussed in school, we have no way of knowing just how they are presented. I feel these things should not be left to chance at all. This is also a good time to reinforce the things that are appropriate – social activities, service projects and parties organized around wholesome themes are okay but pairing off for intimate contact is not.

Farzaneh Knight We told them that if you are with somebody for five minutes and have not influenced them, you can be sure that they will have influenced you. Since peer influence is so powerful, we have told our children that they should lead in that aspect and not be the followers.

Julie Young We have to give them high moral standards and hope that they are secure enough to resist peer pressure and to be strong. It helps to find other Bahá'ís who have children the same age and to reinforce those relationships with good friends who are Bahá'ís.

We had an unofficial rule and this was to never ask permission to do anything in front of your friends! They knew that the consequence of doing this would be that we would answer and they might have to deal with feeling embarrassed in front of their friends. And they always knew better than to ask a friend to ask for them! Just breaking these rules was enough to nullify everything. They were allowed to use us as scapegoats when they weren't allowed to do something or go somewhere. Our children did not go to parties but they were very popular nevertheless. This proves to me that teenagers can be popular without having to attend parties. Parents can be strict and still have popular kids.

THE PRINCIPLES OF CHASTITY AND MODERATION

Irene Dominguez We talk about this a lot. We have study sessions on the writings. We send them to youth conferences and other Bahá'í gatherings. It is important for them to meet other Bahá'í youth and to have friends that share similar standards. We also encourage them to bring their friends home. We teach the Faith to them by lending them books and other material.

What are your rules on watching TV?

Lucy Matthews If something was inappropriate, we turned it off. Our daughter was allowed a half hour of TV when she was small – usually an educational programme. We then turned it off. The exception to that was when the teacher assigned a programme to watch. Then she could watch something in addition to the half hour. As she grew, she was so busy doing other things that she didn't watch much TV. She was far more selective and only watched something that she really wanted to, as opposed to something trashy.

Beth Bishop When they were very young, if something inappropriate came on, I would switch it off. When they were older, I would explain why I disapproved of the content. They all had TVs in their rooms from the age of 12, so I had to trust them somewhat.

Joe and Wilma Thompson We had strict rules about TV. They were allowed one hour a night after homework and after all their chores were completed. We also had programmes that were acceptable and they would choose from these. We tried, especially when they were younger, to watch TV with them and to talk about the programmes. For example, what was your favourite part of a movie and why? What good characteristics did this show demonstrate? Was it a good idea to spend our time watching this? Kids need to relax and just enjoy some things but when appropriate we would try and get a dialogue going. 'What would you do in this situation and why?' They need to know that their opinions are important too!

Bernice McKenzie We intentionally did not have any TV until the children were eight and nine years old. We watched TV together and talked about things. I think we would turn it off if we were all watching something together that was clearly inappropriate. I would hate to be a parent now with all the terrible stuff on TV.

Edyth Lewis When the children were young they were allowed to watch no more than an hour a day. This was not difficult as we lived in a remote area that only had black and white TV – or more accurately grey and grey! They were never allowed to watch TV during the daytime and that rule still applied until they were well into their teens when they watched Saturday morning TV if they had nothing better to do.

I don't think that one could now apply such rules. My guess is that my grandson of 20 months has watched or at least been exposed to more TV than his father was in his first 15 years.

Tanya Charles We let our older children watch TV only occasionally when they were pre-schoolers. When the oldest was in school, we began to watch one funny family show together each week. They were still only watching about one other show each week, sometimes Disney-type movies. Both of the older kids were wonderful at playing together or alone. The third child was one who never played alone very well. I relented and she, as a pre-schooler, watched about an hour of educational TV each day to buy myself some time to get things done.

There are lots of shows, even in prime time, I wouldn't like my kids to see. And equally objectionable are the commercials, both ones that advertise inappropriate shows and those that advertise products. When we do watch something on commercial television, I prefer to record it so we can fast-forward through the commercials. The statistics about the number of hours that children spend watching TV and the number of crimes and acts of violence they

THE PRINCIPLES OF CHASTITY AND MODERATION

see are positively chilling. Just as we are selective about what goes into our kids' bodies and don't let them eat candy for dinner, we are selective about what goes into their minds. And there is room for occasional treats in both areas. If we were to watch a show that was inappropriate, I trust we would stop. Of course, it would be helpful to explain why and to offer an appropriate alternative.

Television viewing can be an emotional issue for parents. Do what seems to work for you and your family. It may help to remember that the television makes a lousy babysitter. Use it to learn and to entertain rather than to fill time and you will be more satisfied.

Andrew Adams Strictly limit TV, especially when the child is young. Have children ask for permission to turn on the TV. They should state how long they want to watch and what they want to watch. Parents must not watch inappropriate programming. You must do what you want your kids to do. Think about how you want your kids to be, then be that way yourself. If you don't want them to smoke, don't smoke. If you don't want them to watch trash on television, don't watch trash on television. Be honest with them. If you secretly smoke or secretly indulge in trash on TV, you are teaching them a much more hurtful practice – dishonesty. You will destroy their trust in you and their respect for you. They will not obey you. You will have lost your position in the family.

Kevin Johnson No TV until their homework was done. Yes, we monitored what they watched. No junk was allowed. If it was inappropriate, we turned it off or switched to something else. There was much less TV watching then.

Phoebe Untekar We monitored somewhat but our kids had pretty good judgement. If a show was inappropriate for them, then it was also inappropriate for us and we simply turned it off.

Celia Stewart One thing that we were absolutely adamant about was the rule to have *no* MTV! We blocked it on the cable. We got a satellite mini dish so we could block all the music channels. We think the videos that go with the music are very harmful!

Paul Oliver We do not have cable, just videos. We consult on how the movie felt from a moral standpoint.

Katayun Golshani My recommendation is that when children are small, you really don't need to put them in front of the TV set. TV should be avoided as much as possible in these early years. What's the rush? It's far preferable that parents remain with their children as much as possible when their children are small. You want the parent/child experience to be an interactive one, rather than the child in isolation with objects on TV. Being there, sitting there, holding them, hugging them and conversing with them are all wonderful things.

As the child gets older, there is no reason why anyone of any age should watch inappropriate programmes or commercials on TV. To me, this means pictures and images that are inappropriate for the soul. It doesn't matter whether it's an adult soul or a child's soul. It's just bad for the soul.

The way the human psyche copes with abrasive material or sexual images is that it becomes desensitized to it. That means that it would no longer register it as abnormal. It becomes unaware of its impact. But that doesn't mean that there is no impact. It's just like when 'Abdu'l-Bahá tells us that the body accustoms itself to poison. He talks about the people who become accustomed to opium so that they are unable to live without it. Why should we accustom our bodies to so much poison? Parents have a responsibility to take charge.

I'm very distressed about the way the movie industry uses words that are insulting to the soul. Four-letter words don't have to be used to make a good movie. Foul language is truly unnecessary.

When they're young, don't expose your children to these things. When they're older and they go to a friend's house, for example,

THE PRINCIPLES OF CHASTITY AND MODERATION

make sure that the family shares the same values and beliefs so that they don't expose your child to bad influences. There is a great advantage in doing other things. If our children watch too much TV, we are in essence depriving them from doing things that are far more worthwhile. More than half an hour a day is truly too much. Watching TV is a very passive thing. We miss opportunities for developing emotional intelligence by watching TV. Oftentimes, when people are watching TV, and guests or friends arrive, nobody makes any form of eye contact, they walk around like zombies and no one greets anyone. There's no conversation, no interaction, no socialization and there's no learning how to give and take. TV really deprives the child of opportunities for emotional growth. We see emotional dummies. This affects many marriages as well as people's abilities to fully use their faculties.

Which was more of a concern - sex and sexual images on TV or violence or both?

Simon Scott Sex and sexual images are always glorified on TV and are the greater problem. See the current list of venereal diseases plaguing the world. Violence is not always glorified and usually people don't dabble in murder for sport.

Edyth Lewis For me violence is more difficult to explain than sex and sexual images but the children were quite old before being exposed to either on TV.
When I was supervisor at a playgroup some of the little boys would go round attacking each other in the name of their cartoon character hero, Hong Kong Phooey. I'm not sure if there would have been fights anyway but sometimes children pick up on the slightest thing and even a cartoon can have an influence.

Linda Bandari Both sex and violence on TV were concerns of mine. Our society has become so violent and I think that it is partly because of what is shown on TV. There are other choices of what to watch. If you cannot find anything appropriate, turn off the TV, read a book, play a game or talk together.

Beth Bishop I would be concerned about both, though I think a lot of teenage boys tend to watch thrillers or violence. If I saw them watching something really nasty I would express my disapproval.

Donna Smith We are afloat in a debased culture. Children are absorbing it from a very young age. Only the home, the Bahá'í community and the Bahá'í schools are striving to maintain the standards of the Faith. As the beloved Guardian said, they must realize the age that they are living in and act in the opposite way.[3]

Lucy Matthews There wasn't much of either in her day, so I really wouldn't know! Boys love violence. It's usually harmless. Sex is more of a concern. Our grandson loves to shoot paintballs. He'll outgrow it. He's a boy.

Tanya Charles Both sexual content and violence are of concern to me. We want our youth to be chaste. We need to consider what messages they are getting on this subject. It seems every role model, in fiction and in real life, sends the message that sex before marriage is okay and fun. It's hard to be the only voice saying, 'Wait'. I like to up the odds by reducing the number of messages coming in that disagree with the principles of the Faith and by increasing the number of messages that support our beliefs. Sadly, we can no longer even go to the mall without being bombarded by sex. Two nationwide chains in the US that sell clothes targeted to youth advertise their spring tops as sexy. The one-shoulder look is in, as are bare midriffs and short, short skirts. I'm not advocating that our girls wear floor-length gowns and veils but modesty is the standard and it is tough for our youth to balance fitting in with peers and the standards of the Faith.

Is there truly a relationship between watching violence and committing violence? It seems both sides can cite 'proof' to support their view. What I think is certain is that being repeatedly exposed to violence can deaden us to the shock of it. And what positive outcome is there from watching it? None that I know of. Once again, if we want the standard to be using consultation as the tool for problem-solving, let's increase the number of examples in our kids' lives showing that and decrease the examples of beating or killing someone who disagrees.

Did you monitor and/or select the music your children listened to?

Even music, art, and literature, which are to represent and inspire the noblest sentiments and highest aspirations and should be a source of comfort and tranquillity for troubled souls, have strayed from the straight path and are now the mirrors of the soiled hearts of this confused, unprincipled, and disordered age.[4]

Fatemeh Pfingston Yes. What music my children listened to, what programme they watched on TV, and who their friends were – these were all monitored in a loving way with open communication.

Celia Stewart I tried to be aware of what they were listening to. No CDs with warnings on them came into the house.

Simon Scott I monitor somewhat and point out that the vast majority of music is written by people whose values are in conflict with the teachings of Bahá'u'lláh.

Farzaneh Knight There was no need to. In fact, my husband was in the music business. He shares with the children many similar tastes in recording artists. They often swap CDs.

Katayun Golshani Unfortunately, music that's out there is like air. It seeps in. When they're young, you can obviously monitor and supervise the music. You're the one who's in charge and buying everything. As they get older, they'll be the ones choosing the music that they like. You don't have the ability to be there all the time. Ideally, you talk about the principle that what one hears and sees is not going to be insignificant. These things affect us and stay with us. The lyrics, the beat and all these things are of significance. My suggestion is to accustom children early on to the classical music of any culture. If good music is accompanied by good lyrics, it's even better. 'Abdu'l-Bahá suggested that children should have training in music. They are then able to be connoisseurs of good music. Music is supposed to be a ladder for the soul. We want to make sure that when we hear music, we are elevated. Recognize the power that music has in order to develop awareness so that we can become wise consumers of good music rather than blind consumers of whatever they sell us or whatever is played out there.

Kevin Johnson They selected. We monitored. When the lyrics were gross, we didn't allow them to be played.

John and Barbara Hartley No, we did not. We might comment on a selection or ask that the volume be lowered but that was not a concern.

Michelle Sharpe No. Unfortunately they moved a little too quickly for us on this one. They had already decided who was 'cool'. However, when we listened to the words and the messages we explained quite a bit. They became aware of the context. Sadly, Nancy mentioned that, for the most part, any music that she liked had foul language. Now that she is getting older, I have noticed that she is making better choices, choosing more middle-of-the-road easy listening as opposed to the popular stuff.

Linda Bandari I did not monitor or select the music that my children listened to but could not help hearing what they played most of the time. The music that they chose to listen to was not always appealing to me but not too objectionable.

Tom and Andrea Edwards MTV was limited. When particular

songs were inappropriate, we had them turn away from the TV or radio station and we then expressed our opinions.

What are your rules on clothes?

Such a chaste and holy life, with its implications of modesty, purity, temperance, decency, and clean-mindedness, involves no less than the exercise of moderation in all that pertains to dress, language, amusements, and all artistic and literary avocations.[5]

The world must see that, regardless of each passing whim or current fashion of the generality of mankind, the Bahá'í lives his life according to the tenets of his Faith. We must not allow the fear of rejection by our friends and neighbours to deter us from our goal to live the Bahá'í life.[6]

Tanya Charles At least violence on TV can be turned off but sexy items in store windows are everywhere. It's not a good idea and it can even be dangerous to let children and teenagers dress in a sexy manner. We always shop together. We have explained to our daughters why revealing clothes can be problematic and we have told her that we will not buy her clothes that bring her unsafe attention. Our strategy has always been to compromise on one *little* thing, such as a pair of earrings that she might really like. We have told our daughters that if they are dressed immodestly, people will have inappropriate and immodest thoughts about them. Thoughts follow actions. Immodest thoughts will attract the wrong kind of people, thoughts and actions. They have been taught that they need to dress in a manner that engenders respect.

Donald Pope Nothing outlandish. They are representing God's chosen ones everywhere. People will judge the Faith by them. Everything matters.

Lucy Matthews I would not allow T-shirts with questionable logos and messages. But you have to be somewhat flexible. Modesty is not a question of morality, it's a question of what's acceptable. Don't be a plaything of the ignorant. I would not allow the skimpiest bikini. You have to be reasonable. Don't be extreme. Don't go around forbidding things. But you also have to say to your children, 'Let's not have people look at you and say, "Oh, what a stupid girl or what an idiot boy".'

John and Barbara Hartley If the clothes were neat and clean, it was okay. Neither of them favoured extremely baggy clothes. On occasion, we did tell them not to buy certain T-shirts but that was not an issue most of the time. Fads such as caps on sideways or backwards are harmless and if they wanted to wear them that way, it was okay.

Michelle Sharpe We always expect modesty and appropriate clothing. We have discouraged miniskirts and short shorts. And we have always encouraged one-piece swimsuits. Our daughter recently purchased a very modest two-piece/tankini. She understood the reason why we said nothing skimpy or revealing. I think that when children understand the 'why,' they will be able to make the right choices. It is really important that they understand the wisdom behind the rules. If we can teach them the wisdom of practising modesty and chastity, then we will have done our part.

Donna Smith This is a step-by-step process. It is a learning process. Little by little. Take it one step at a time. You'll get there.

Todd and Debbie McEwen We have no specific rules, but encourage 'moderation in all that pertains to dress'.[7] In particular, we would strongly discourage any clothes designed to be sexually provocative – however, this tends to be a fashion more with girls than boys, and having all boys, this has not been an issue. As a teacher of Bahá'í children's classes, Todd has had to discuss the appropriateness of the clothes that some of the girls chose to wear – which have sometimes been over-revealing.

THE PRINCIPLES OF CHASTITY AND MODERATION

Tom and Andrea Edwards Questionable logos would be banned. Tight jeans or sweaters and miniskirts were discouraged. Many of our discussions were about a matter of degree, such as of tightness or shortness. Discussions were frequent.

Richard and Theresa Baker Our daughter enjoyed wearing miniskirts and bikinis and not always appropriate clothes (in our opinion). However, it was never so bad that we couldn't laugh about or give advice to her (not generally taken)!
Our son was never keen on wearing questionable clothes. Probably the fact that he always wanted to be an airline pilot – and achieved his ambition – had something to do with generally wanting to look well turned out and not too extraordinary.

Farzaneh Knight No skimpy bikinis but we did allow two-pieces, since we live in the tropics. No exaggerated miniskirts. We have reminded them that chastity includes the way one dresses and that one can be attractive and elegant without being provocative and giving out mixed messages.

Paul Oliver All these rules were looked at from the standpoint of helping them make decisions on the appropriateness of carrying the message of Bahá'u'lláh.

Katayun Golshani The way we dress ourselves sends a message. Bahá'u'lláh tells us that we should not make ourselves 'the playthings of the ignorant'.[8] You don't want to be dressed in such a way that when people pass you by, they turn around to take another look at you. That means that you're attracting attention in the wrong way. Dressing sends a message as to who you are and what you want people to look at. The way you dress draws attention to certain aspects of yourself. Dress is not just something benign. One has to appreciate the kind of message one sends by the clothes one chooses to wear.
One also has to consider that dress is a cultural thing. One needs to ask oneself, 'Within this environment, who do I want to

be and what kind of a message do I want to send with my clothing? Where do I want the attention of people who look at me to be focused?' Then one can decide, 'Do I want to wear a miniskirt and why? How short should it be?' Discussing it is essential.

What would you do if your teenager wanted to get a tattoo?

Katayun Golshani When youth have a Bahá'í identity, they generally think fairly globally. They're aware of the worth of their ability to move around the world and to relate to people of different cultures and backgrounds. They are aware of the worth of having to earn the respect of people of different backgrounds and cultures. Once you know that, the question becomes, 'What kind of message do you give to people in different parts of the world if you have a tattoo?' Many cultures consider them to be very degrading symbols. For example, in many parts of the world tattoos are only for people who are not very respectable. For them, it's not an issue of decoration. It's an issue of who you are and what kind of values you project. So you set yourself up for being judged outwardly because of this permanent decoration that you put on yourself. The question is, 'Do you want to have a permanent mark that would repel a group of people that you might find important, that you might want to connect, teach, guide and help with whatever?' Once you speak to youth about these things on these terms, youth generally say no, they don't want to pay that kind of price for this decoration. They don't want to do something permanent that limits them in their ability to serve.

Whatever we do with our appearance is a way of communicating and sending a message. What are we saying by sending this message?

I would bring these things up as points of discussion. I would bring documentary videos and research. And then ask them, 'When we know all these things, how do we want to look? How do we want to be? How do we want to present ourselves?' My preference for youth is that they not limit themselves through their appearance and that they are able to serve.

THE PRINCIPLES OF CHASTITY AND MODERATION

Donna Smith I would read him the *Kitáb-i-Aqdas*. If he still remained adamant, I would encourage him to get one that is temporary and that could be removed.

John and Barbara Hartley Neither boy ever expressed an interest in tattoos, although I spoke to them a couple times about it because my brother has them and they asked why I didn't. I told them I was never interested and that my brother now wishes he hadn't got them. If they asked to have them, I would probably ask why and would talk about the permanency of the procedure. Earrings (which they don't have) can be taken out but tattoos are not so easily removed. We never indulged the kids when they wanted to adopt trends just because their friends did something.

Richard and Theresa Baker We used to speak about such things as they were growing up. We would advise against getting tattoos, saying that they might like it at the time but they would have to live with it and it wasn't advisable. One day our daughter came home saying she had had a tattoo (just to see our reactions I think)! I held my breath and kept quiet while my husband got quite agitated! She then showed us that it was a temporary tattoo and we breathed a sigh of relief! She was just testing us!

Bernice McKenzie I hope I would not allow it. I think Bahá'u'lláh's admonition that we do not become a plaything of the ignorant is the principle here.

Margerie Gibson No. No permanent disfiguring marks allowed. If she ever asks, I will point out to her that when she was four years old, she would have chosen a childish character for a tattoo. I will then ask her if she would still like that today. After her rather emphatic 'NO!' I will ask her what makes her think her tastes won't change just as dramatically in the *next* five years?

Nina Sadaghiyan I would not allow it. Tattoos are a form of submitting to peer pressure.

Donald Pope Remind them that they represent Bahá'u'lláh on earth.

What would you do if your teenager wanted to have his tongue, nose or navel pierced?

> The choice of clothing and the cut of the beard and its dressing are left to the discretion of men. But beware, O people, lest ye make yourselves the playthings of the ignorant.[9]

Farzaneh Knight When you teach your children about the nobility of man and about human dignity, these things are not only unattractive, they are just not a part of their lives. Thank God we were saved from this because they both take a very dim view of that kind of thing. On the contrary, our daughters are both very elegant, stylish and poised.

Edyth Lewis I have never seen the attractiveness of having bits and bobs pierced. However, the only thing that I have found in the Bahá'í writings that relates vaguely to this issue is in the seventh Glad-Tiding: 'The choice of clothing and the cut of the beard and its dressing are left to the discretion of men. But beware, O people, lest ye make yourselves the playthings of the ignorant.'[10]

In the case of teenagers, 'the ignorant' are much more likely to make fun of one of their peers who is dressed in a suit than they are to someone who has bits of metal attached to anything that it can be attached to, bright orange hair and a heart-shaped tattoo on his arm.

All my children have had their ears pierced. Against my wishes, the two younger ones had their ears pierced while they were on holiday with their grandmother who went and checked the place out before allowing them to go in.

I think parents have to stand back and ask themselves: 'Does this really matter? Is this against the principles of the Faith? Is this a passing fad that they will grow out of?' More than anything, parents find their children's dress embarrassing but this is something that will pass and they will turn into people who wear what is conventional regardless.

Beth Bishop Two of them had various piercings though we were not really in favour of that (except for ears). But they can be removed any time.

Lucy Matthews No, I would not allow it. Having your ears pierced as a female is acceptable. All the rest of it is ridiculous. Don't scar yourself where it's going to show for the rest of your life. Don't become a plaything of the ignorant. You'll regret all this.

Paul Oliver Definitely not until they were 18. They could then choose legally. Until then, we are responsible for them. Tattoos and these sorts of piercings are a desecration of the human temple.

Todd and Debbie McEwen We would consult and strongly discourage it. However, as they get older we let them make more choices themselves. We have to remain flexible depending on what they want to do, whether we believe they fully understand the consequences of what they want to do and how mature we feel they are.

Nina Sadaghiyan No. The body is the temple of the soul and needs to be treated with respect.

Joe and Wilma Thompson Fortunately, they were adults before this became the rage. Although this is not permanent, they need to think about the message they are sending to people.

Richard and Theresa Baker I think it's hard to say *not* to do these things but *important* to give reasons as they grow up as to why you don't think it's a good idea. However, a lot of these things are fashionable at a given moment among their peers and sometimes they also may decide to have a go. Our daughter came home one day with her navel pierced and a pretty stone inserted there! I had been briefed beforehand but my husband gasped with shock when he unexpectedly saw it! But, as my daughter said to us, she doesn't smoke, doesn't drink alcohol, doesn't take drugs, doesn't have sex outside marriage – so surely having her navel pierced isn't such a big deal!! We agreed.

Grace Simpson No, I would not allow it. The writings tell us not to make ourselves playthings for others. Luckily she never wanted to do this.

Melissa Taheri I would oppose this on medical grounds as well as socially. How one feels at 17 or 18 is often not what one feels as an adult. Piercings would make it more difficult to get a job. Neither tattoos nor piercings have been an issue. Both boys are opposed to pain and I don't think either ever considered doing it.

Michelle Sharpe Our teenage daughter has hinted that she would like to have body piercing. We have totally discouraged it. I am somewhat okay with an earring for our son. I certainly would not be the one to promote it. I am okay with some things that are presented in a respectful way. My children are very quick to tell me that I should not judge someone by their outward look. I must say that I agree. However, I will always expect that they would not dress to offend in any way. Flexibility is important.

Donald Pope Remind your child that he represents Bahá'u'lláh on earth.

Simon Scott No, absolutely not! This is a crass act of counter-culture, 'in your face' rebellion and peer pressure. No to piercing, tattoos or any other to-be invented fads that are intended to differentiate, on the most superficial level, one generation from another. There is no need to be tolerant of the standards of a decadent age.[11] If children want to differentiate themselves from my generation, then they should do something that leads to their own and society's improvement, not something that is merely conformist rebellion.

If this were to happen, the level of in-house restriction, punishment and so on would be quite a bit stronger. I am a believer in 'tough love', not permissive indulgence.

What is your policy about hairstyles? What if your teenager wanted to dye his hair purple?

Donna Smith No. Only that Bahá'u'lláh said: 'Let there be naught in your demeanour of which sound and upright minds would disapprove, and make not yourselves the playthings of the ignorant.'[12] Kids today might not necessarily look particularly strange with their hair dyed purple or with spikes. This is no problem for me, as long as they don't become the object of laughter or ridicule. A teenager is capable of learning how he wants to express himself. All the real work of parenting is done in early childhood. By the time the child is a teen, hair colour is a very minor issue. The reality is his character, not the colour of his hair.

Angela Brown We have talked with our 15 year old son about those writings in which Bahá'u'lláh has given us permission to adorn ourselves, as long as we don't pass the point of moderation and make ourselves 'the playthings of the ignorant'. Our response to his questions regarding dying his hair and tattooing have been that it is only to be allowed as long as it is not permanent, not contradicting the teachings and only done during vacation time rather than school time.

Kevin Johnson During the 1960s, all four of our sons decided that they wanted long hair. We said, 'Okay,' just as long as it was clean and combed. The girls picked whatever style they liked. We would have allowed purple or spikes. But it never came up. Hair grows out and there's no danger.

Paul Oliver Definitely not until they were 18. They could then choose legally. Until then, we are responsible for them. At least hair colour is not permanent.

Fatemeh Pfingston Hairstyle was never a problem in our family but if my child wanted to dye her hair purple, I simply would not allow it.

Beth Bishop Hair colour is a matter of fashion. My daughter always used to colour her hair before big Bahá'í events when she would see her friends. My son had dreadlocks for a while. Teenagers always follow strange fashions, and as long as they are firm in the Faith and not indecent, it seems a minor thing.

Bernice McKenzie Youth is a time for experimentation (within reason). It's only hair.

Tom and Andrea Edwards This would have to be weighed with each individual situation. In some instances, we would consider the principle of 'choosing your battles'.

Joe and Wilma Thompson Although this is not permanent, they need to think about the message they are sending to people.

Linda Bandari My children were never interested in dying their hair different colours or getting it cut in wild styles. During the summer they would put lemon juice in their hair and sit outside in the sun to add highlights to their hair and did I not object to that. If my children had wanted to dye their hair different colours, I would have tried to discourage them. If they insisted, I might have agreed to let them do it, for example, for the weekend. I found that oftentimes my children would say that they wanted to do something that I might not particularly like just to get a reaction out of me but if I didn't make a big deal out of it, they ended up deciding not to do it after all.

THE PRINCIPLES OF CHASTITY AND MODERATION

If you ever suspected that your child had been drinking alcohol, taking drugs or sniffing glue, how would you deal with this?

... in the 'Book of Aqdas' we are definitely forbidden to take not only wine, but every thing that deranges the mind.[13]

... Bahá'ís should not use hallucinogenic agents, including LSD, peyote and similar substances, except when prescribed for medical treatment.[14]

Katayun Golshani Oh boy! If I ever suspected that, we would go to a counsellor immediately! This should not be taken lightly at all. The child needs professional help in order to find out what to do about it. I would seek a counsellor who knows the serious impact of drugs and how to deal with this sort of thing. I would prefer a counsellor who has a spiritual awareness with regard to these issues. This is a spiritual issue. I would look at the whole make-up of the friends that my child is hanging out with and the environment. I would turn every stone to see why and how this could be changed and reversed. I would do everything.

Lucy Matthews We gave her lots of self esteem. We made her know that the soul is connected to the body. You treat it with respect. Bahá'u'lláh emphasized that over and over again. We were born noble. Children should never be taught that they were born in sin. Bahá'ís approach things in a far more positive way. Our daughter felt different and isolated when growing up. It bothered her. But she was also very happy and self-assured in other ways. I think all teens go through similar phases and go through periods of insecurity. But she had very firm moral values. She was a great kid!

Tom and Andrea Edwards Pull in the reins.

Margerie Gibson I would sit down with her and her father in a family consultation, ask leading questions about what she was trying to get out of the experiences emotionally and provide her with as many concrete examples as possible of the damage to her life that would result from continued use.

Mostly I don't expect it to happen. There are so many people near us in our family and neighbourhood that exemplify the disaster that drugs and alcohol make of your life that Kendra already has a healthy distaste for that aspect of 'fun'.

Linda Bandari If I suspected that my children had been drinking alcohol, taking drugs or sniffing glue, I would confront them. There are usually telltale signs if you are looking for them. I always purposely stayed awake until my children came home at night and talked to them to see how their evening went. Sometimes I called to see if they were at the house they said they were going to be at, and so on. I felt that it was my responsibility as a parent to keep my children safe and not let them get into too much trouble.

Todd and Debbie McEwen We have never suspected them of these things. If we did, we would first ask them if it were true and if it was we would consult with them about what the Bahá'í writings say. We would also consult the appropriate authorities and support agencies.

Kevin Johnson This didn't happen. If it had, I would have tried to find out why. I would have used every means to stop it. I would become more involved in the child's life.

Simon Scott The twin pillars of 'reward and retribution'.[15] This is retribution time – but after I ascertained to my satisfaction their reason for having done this.

5

School and Peer-Related Issues

Were you selective about the friends that your children made?

The company of the ungodly increaseth sorrow, whilst fellowship with the righteous cleanseth the rust from off the heart.[1]

Andrew Adams If the child's friends begin to have more influence than you do as a parent, it is time to cut down on the amount of time the child spends with those friends and increase the amount of time the child spends with you. The child will not like this at first but you must be firm. He will understand later.

Often, Bahá'í kids are singled out by kids at school who are bullies. The innate goodness of the Bahá'í child is perceived by the bully as a threat. Sometimes our Bahá'í children are fascinated by the power of the evil behaviour and are attracted to the bully. Our child either becomes the target of the bully or befriends the bully and then, having been negatively affected, seeks to become like the bully. We need to be aware of this and educate our children about it. Sooner or later, I have found, that given a strong Bahá'í foundation, our kids will choose good kids like themselves as friends.

Of course, as kids get older, their peers may try to corrupt them. We need to be vigilant parents who directly supervise our kids during non-school hours.

Julie Young We were very selective. Typically what happened was that our children became friends with people whose parents we knew and who we were willing to have our children be with.

When the children were young (elementary school age), we would invite parents to birthday parties. We would send out invitations to the kids and put a little note inviting the parents too. We would also do this for Halloween (showing them that our home was a safe, wholesome place – in fact, our home developed a great reputation every Halloween and lots of people would come over!). We would sometimes do this for Ayyám-i-Há but parents would rarely come to that unless we had already made a strong connection. So basically, we would invite parents to our home at least twice a year – birthdays and Halloween.

As our children got older, we would invite their friends over and see if we cared for them. Later on, we would invite their parents. Shortly before our children entered their teen years, we became very actively involved in PTA and school athletics. We got a chance to know all the parents. When our daughter's friends were not desirable, they were wise enough to 'leave them be'. I usually knew if any kid was going 'down hill' or 'off the deep end'. However, it was not so easy with our son. He accused me of backbiting when I heard about one of his friends behaving in a highly undesirable way. I told him that he needed to figure out a way to disassociate himself from this friend. The friend came over to our house and wanted to go out with him. So our son told him that he was busy. He learned but he needed some prodding from us!

Irene Dominguez Yes, we have been selective. The parent needs to tell the child that he is special and that we even need to select friends that are better than ourselves in order for us to learn from them.

Michelle Sharpe Yes, we made a big effort to get to know the parents and their families. We made a point of inviting friends to our home first to see how things worked out. My children were great judges of character. If any kid was mean, lied or was a bullying type, our children dropped him immediately. We taught our children to be kind and caring with friends and to expect the same from them. It usually worked.

SCHOOL AND PEER-RELATED ISSUES

Todd and Debbie McEwen We have not stopped them from making friends with anyone and would not do so unless there was an extremely good reason to prevent the friendship. They have learned from experience how to select friends. Now that they are older, they are generally very sensible in their choice.

Linda Bandari I was not selective about the friends that my kids had. My children were always encouraged to invite their friends to our house. That way I was able to get to know their friends too. I also tried to get to know the parents of the kids that my children wanted to spend time with. This was no small task as my children went to private school and had friends all over the city. My children usually realized themselves that some of their friends had better habits than others and chose to spend time with those with similar beliefs.

John and Barbara Hartley We associated with the parents of the friends we wanted our children to be friends with. We asked our children if they enjoyed the way in which certain children behaved, and if they didn't, we suggested they did not spend much time with them.

George and Mary Burke Our children have been taught to see themselves as part of a family, that they have rights and responsibilities in that family. The friends they choose are brought into the family circle and become part of maintaining the unity of the family. If their friends influence them in such a way that they lose sight of who they are and what they are trying to accomplish, or if a friend exerts a negative influence on our child, then that relationship is brought to a close. Conversely, we encourage our children to develop relationships that will grow. That requires bringing them into our family activities and gatherings. This has proved to be a wise strategy.

Once children start school and enter middle childhood (ages six and up), they start to undergo tremendous peer pressure. How can we minimize this? How can we teach our Bahá'í children to be leaders instead of followers?

Donna Smith By watching their physical, emotional and spiritual health like a hawk. You know your children from birth. You know signs of ill health in any of these areas. Pay attention and correct it when it happens because it will happen. Be confident that you are doing what is the very best for your children, even though they may not always believe it. You are responsible to God for raising them. You are not responsible to your children. They are responsible to you. You are the intermediary between them and God when they are young and it is you who gradually teaches them that their true strength lies in reliance on God. Your children will learn it from you trusting the writings and trusting yourself.

Beth Bishop By inviting their friends to the house so they can see how you live. By encouraging friendships with other Bahá'í youth. By encouraging the child to teach the Faith and to be prepared to be different, though not necessarily in an open way all the time.

Lucy Matthews The child has to know that he will be under peer pressure and that we do not agree with all of the actions and attitudes around us. I think a Bahá'í child simply absorbs so much from his parents. We're not even aware of what we're giving them. Back in the 1950s we were driving through a black neighbourhood in Birmingham, Alabama, with our daughter and her best friend who was not a Bahá'í. They were very young – this was before they were even eight years old. Her best friend looked out of the window and used a negative racial slur. Our daughter was appalled and immediately corrected her. She told her that it was mean and insulting. Her friend never forgot it. We give our children things that we don't know that we're giving them. They also need to have these things put into words. You can also explain things whenever the occasion arises.

SCHOOL AND PEER-RELATED ISSUES

Linda Bandari I have found that the best way to help children to undergo the peer pressure or any other problems is to listen to them and keep an open line of communication. Don't push them away because you are busy or distracted. Let them know that you will always be there for them and follow through on whatever you say. I tried never to make a promise that I could not keep. Giving them that safety net of knowing that they can count on your help if they need it gives them the strength to get through problems they encounter. I have heard kids say that their parents say one thing but do another or that they are too busy to listen to them. This does not build a trusting relationship.

Bernice McKenzie If the children know they are Baháʼís and are exposed to a good Baháʼí environment in the home and the community, the peer pressure will not be so awful. However, if the home and the community are not places of sanctuary, then it will be very difficult for the children.

John and Barbara Hartley Encourage the child to tell the parents what is being said in school. Explain the reasons for allowing or not allowing them to do what their friends are doing.

Michelle Sharpe By not having a big emphasis on material items and showing our children how to be happy without having to get something. Pay close attention to the music, games and shows that can be such a huge influence. Sit and watch with them. Discuss the stereotyping or overemphasis on the material stuff. TV plays a huge part in peer pressure. Parents can contribute more by ensuring that the spiritual development of the child always comes first. Encourage your children to carefully watch the examples that they follow. Music has such negatives statements, words and explicit sexuality. This music is sung by teens who sometimes do not even hear the lyrics. Our son arrived home one day with a song 'that had a real ring to it and a nice beat'. He shared how 'the rhyming was so cool'. I looked at the printout that he had and was horrified at the lyrics. They could not have been more graphic, explicit and full of sexism.

Kids see the singers in their cool outfits and they do not realize what is truly being portrayed. Parents often do not pay attention to the details. Our daughter has basically told me, 'Mom, there is not too much music today without four-letter words, sex and violence.'

Parents truly need to play a more active role in their child's development. We have been too busy with other stuff. Some of it has been well intentioned. When our children are raised spiritually they will be more confident. They will then be 'the peer pressure'.

Simon Scott Peer pressure is a huge challenge but then it always has been. The teaching of real standards of what is right versus what is wrong has to be clear in a child's mind. The writings from Bahá'u'lláh to the Universal House of Justice give more than enough information as to what is or is not allowed. If that is clear in a child's mind, you have the beginnings of what was once called 'a conscience' to help guide him in his individual choices. Beyond that, it is the force of example. The parents must live along the lines of what they teach. If the children respect and want to emulate a good example, then that is great. Otherwise, there is a problem.

Andrew Adams There is no escaping peer pressure. We can only work through it a day at a time. Every day we must reorient ourselves to our Creator. As parents, peer pressure affects us too. We must have the courage not to give in to peer pressure. Our kids will learn from our example. Let them choose friends to play with. You determine which ones you will allow them to play with. Evaluate their friends. Evaluate their friends' parents.

What were your rules on slumber parties and sleep-overs?

Andrew Adams We do not want our children staying overnight at other people's homes, period. With all the alcohol, drugs and molestation, why risk your child's future? We only allow our children to sleep at family members' houses. If a friend is having a

SCHOOL AND PEER-RELATED ISSUES

slumber party, we let our kids attend but we pick them up at 9:00. They sleep at home in their own beds.

Edyth Lewis It was only my daughter who went on sleep-overs from about the age of 12 and had a few of her own. I knew where she was going and no worries that she would come to harm. Not only would she say her own prayers but she would make sure that her non-Bahá'í friends said them too!

Farzaneh Knight Yes. They had tons of them. Mostly at our house! They always took their prayer books themselves. Their friends had parents supervising and all conditions were met satisfactorily for us.

Angela Brown I was not crazy about my children going to other homes to sleep over, unless I knew the families fairly well and was sure that my children would be well protected from harmful influences and behaviours. The more stories in recent years regarding sex abuse, pornography and children walking the streets at night unaccompanied by adults, the more concerned I have become! Yet children immensely enjoy such activities, so I try to be moderate and reasonable. I was under pressure to get to know my children's friends' families so that I would be better prepared to make a fair decision. I didn't allow my children to stay overnight in a home where the family members flagrantly cursed, drank, smoked or took drugs. In talking over these standards with one's child, the child becomes more committed and aware of the standards as well, using them to consider whether a parent will allow him to stay overnight with a particular friend or to have him over.

I also told my children that if they asked such questions in front of their friends they would be told 'no' outright, as such a question would necessitate a private conversation between parent and child. In this way there would be less opportunity for embarrassment of one of my children's friends in the event I had to say 'no'.

As far as age is concerned, this really depends on a particular child's maturity and willingness to play host in a courteous and hospitable way.

Overall, because of the opportunity for influencing character, I really prefer that overnights be primarily with Bahá'í children or Bahá'í-like children.

Richard and Theresa Baker This is a tricky question! We allowed a few sleep-over parties in our house. However, we discovered on one occasion that my daughter's school friends (aged about 15–16) did not respect the fact that we wanted to sleep and they made a lot of noise. One of my daughter's friends even had a small bottle of alcohol with her. That was a distressing time. We talked to the half a dozen friends of my daughter about our feelings but they didn't really appreciate them. Our daughter was embarrassed by the behaviour of her friends and wasn't particularly interested in having more sleep-overs.

We were not keen on them sleeping at their friends' homes, however, but we generally allowed it if they insisted they wanted to go and as long as they could promise good behaviour. They knew we trusted them.

With their Bahá'í friends it was quite different. They knew what was expected of them and they used to have a lot of fun together. They would bring sleeping bags with them and mostly talk all night! As Bahá'ís together, they would encourage each other in saying prayers. With their non-Bahá'í friends I don't expect they did remember to say their prayers but then we often forget to say prayers in such circumstances too!

George and Mary Burke We don't allow sleep-overs as a general rule and our children don't question our authority on this issue. They are occasionally allowed to sleep over at their cousin's house, as family is different. Our reasoning is simple: they don't need to sleep with their friends; it fulfils no fruitful purpose that can't be accomplished during the daylight hours.

Donna Smith With boys these are not so common. The one time we did let our youngest go we regretted it because they watched absolutely horrible scary movies all night long (he was 12 or 13 at the time). It had a very bad effect on him for quite some time. That was the last sleep-over he was able to go to. We elected to be the bad guys so he didn't lose face and that was fine. He was secretly relieved.

If I had to do it again, I would be very, very careful. I would grill the host parents (politely of course), and if I felt uneasy, I would be the big 'meanie' and say no. A sleep-over has to be a point of reassurance in the parent's heart.

All children come up with 'But all my friends do it' for everything that parents don't allow them to do. If you have your well-thought-out reasons, there is no discussion. Case closed. As Bahá'í parents we are constantly teaching our children consultation, trust and so on. When push comes to shove, my feeling is that your word is law until they are 15. That sounds autocratic. I am talking about the bottom line. All the time you are training them, you are opening up boundaries so that when they are ready, they will be educated and balanced adults. So 'your law' is most of the time in the background as you are always gently encouraging them into independence and making decisions and making mistakes and learning from them.

As to their saying prayers, I would talk with the parents and see what their attitude was. If I were not impressed, I would counsel the child to go to a private place and say them in his mind.

Katayun Golshani My children were never very far from my sight. If we had parties, they were generally during the day. When they wanted to stay overnight somewhere – which was extremely rare – we told them that they had to wait until they were older. If they were going to stay with someone, it had to be with a family that we felt very close to. As a rule, I never allowed them to stay over at anyone's house for slumber parties. This was because of the things that I had heard and learned about from my own experience. The rule in our house was that you could go to the birthday party until everyone wanted to go to bed and then you were to come home. I would then pick them up. Our children were sometimes unhappy about that. But it never became an issue. We made sure that they had fun, happiness and joy at other times. We attended Baháʼí schools every summer and winter. They had a chance to be with other friends.

Your pre-teen daughter comes home from school and is devastated that a friend has shunned her and that she feels excluded from a certain group. How do you help her?

George and Mary Burke This has happened and I explained to her that it will happen again. We talked about the reasons why she was shunned and pointed out how many of her friends had always supported her. The important thing, I said, is to leave the conversation knowing that people will disappoint and hurt us but that we must not return the gesture, now that we know how bad it feels.

Lucy Matthews You have to keep the lines of communication open so that your child can feel free and comforted. Children always need comforting. Now ask her what brought it about, what the causes are, why your child is being shunned and so on. Perhaps your child is being shunned by a friend because the friend feels that she will be more popular. There are always bullies and the in-groups can be very mean to one another. I was mean sometimes too. I was just caught up with that peer pressure. It really was a question of maturity. Later I could look back with deep remorse and ask myself how I could have done that, or said that, or treated that girl that way. Even Baháʼí kids can be very cliquey at times. These things should be part of youth training and talked about in all youth sessions. They need to face up and recognize what they're doing. Baháʼís should not be guilty of this. A comment can seem funny at the moment but can be cutting and really hurt someone. If it happens to your daughter, if she is on the receiving end of it, it hurts. You have to talk to her. Then tell her that now that she knows what it feels like, she should be very careful never to do it to anyone else.

Linda Bandari If my daughter came home from school devastated that a friend had shunned her, I would listen and be sympathetic and ask if there was anything I could do to help. I might tell her a similar story of what happened to me and how I felt or what I did. I would indicate that even a friend might do or say things that are hurtful. I might suggest that she invite over one of her other friends or do something fun with someone else to lessen her hurt feelings. I have found that sometimes offering a shoulder to cry on is all that is needed.

Grace Simpson I always taught her to be a Baháʾí. From that point, the child will be isolated by some. I always told her to take the higher road, that things would work out and they did. She respected my opinions when these things turned out the way I said they would.

Paul Oliver This is part of the reality of being a Baháʾí. It is like swimming upstream against a very powerful current. So part of it is helping her to become accustomed to the hardship of isolation that a high standard has. If there is a support group of like-minded youth, it is a huge help. This is a topic for consultation between parent and child.

Donna Smith I would tell her about her soul. I would talk to her about the persecutions of ʿAbduʾl-Bahá as a child and how the Guardian also had to suffer. I would tell her to pray when in these situations and how to nurture herself as best she can and to find new friends and exciting things to do for herself. Then I would talk about sorrow coming from the material world and not the world of the spirit and how no human being escapes sorrow. Most of all, I would emphasize that Baháʾuʾlláh is always with her and show her writings to this effect. Then I would listen to her and watch for what lightens her heart. She will recover. I would then tell her it is a strengthening process and that some day she will appreciate this. I would tell her to be aware when she sees anyone else being treated this way and to show kindness to this person.

Tom and Andrea Edwards Really just try to support her and find ways to help her nurture other friends.

Simon Scott I focus very much on early Christianity. The early Christians were always repudiated and rejected, yet they still had the strength of character that ultimately influenced their neighbours and converted them to Jesus. Bahá'ís can do the same. I therefore focus very much on early Christianity.

Irene Dominguez I would encourage her to look for friends that are more like her. There are always more friends available. I would explain that difficulties always exist. We have to learn how to deal with them. I would tell her that she is very special and that these things happen.

Your child gets bullied, picked on or teased. What do you do?

> Regarding your question about children fighting: the statement of the Master, not to strike back, should not be taken so extremely literally that Bahá'í children must accept to be bullied and thrashed. If they can manage to show a better way of settling disputes than by active self-defence, they should naturally do so.[2]

A Story of 'Abdu'l-Bahá's Childhood I have heard the Most Great Branch, who in those days was a child of only eight years of age, recount one of His experiences as He ventured to leave the house in which He was then residing. 'We had sought shelter', He told us, 'in the house of My uncle, Mírzá Ismá'íl. Ṭihrán was in the throes of the wildest excitement. I ventured at times to sally forth from that house and to cross the street on My way to the market. I would hardly cross the threshold and step into the street, when boys of My age, who were running about, would crowd around Me crying, "Bábí! Bábí!" Knowing well the state of excitement into which all the inhabitants of the capital, both young and old, had fallen, I would deliberately ignore their clamour and quietly steal away to

My home. One day I happened to be walking alone through the market on My way to My uncle's house. As I was looking behind Me, I found a band of little ruffians running fast to overtake Me. They were pelting Me with stones and shouting menacingly, "Bábí! Bábí!" To intimidate them seemed to be the only way I could avert the danger with which I was threatened. I turned back and rushed towards them with such determination that they fled away in distress and vanished. I could hear their distant cry, "The little Bábí is fast pursuing us! He will surely overtake and slay us all!" As I was directing my steps towards home, I heard a man shouting at the top of his voice: "Well done, you brave and fearless child! No one of your age would ever have been able, unaided, to withstand their attack!" From that day onward, I was never again molested by any of the boys of the streets, nor did I hear any offensive word fall from their lips.'[3]

Harriet Douglas My daughters had this happen to them. I would tell them to talk about their pain and frustration and invite them to consult and brainstorm as to the best course of action. I would support the course of action that they thought was best. I would read them stories about 'Abdu'l-Bahá and how He dealt with this. He didn't allow Himself to be victimized and He didn't victimize others. Being spiritual does not mean being a wimp! I would encourage participation in martial arts training – especially akido, karate or judo. This training concentrates on self-control and discipline, bringing about a confidence and self-presentation that makes it less likely that they'll be victimized. The training allows them to counter any attack – physical or emotional – in a strong, peaceful, self-assured, effective manner.

Lucy Matthews The bully has to know what he's doing and he has to be brought up short. In the event of bullying, you have to see to it that the bully knows what he's doing and that there are repercussions for bullying. You'll have to go to the school administration or the child's parents or whatever. It must be stopped. 'Noble have I created thee, yet thou hast abased thyself.'[4] You tell your child that the bully is abasing himself. It hurts him spiritually to allow him to continue. We have to stop him. It is very important that the bully is stopped.

Irene Dominguez Teach her to defend herself in a non-aggressive way, by using the right choice of words, for example. If the bullying occurs at school, the teacher should be told.

Donald Pope If you are going to be spiritual in today's world you'd better be strong – not tough but strong. The parents' task is to awaken the spiritual gifts a child was given and make her strong enough to hold firm to principle regardless of what confronts her. When a child is bullied, you want your child to be strong enough to be assertive, to stand up for what is right. The assertive stand will often put a bully at bay. They are looking for victims. Walking away and ignoring the intimidation can be forms of assertiveness if done from understanding rather than fear. Suggesting to a teacher that a bully might need help may be another form of assertiveness. If the child is not strong enough to take that step, then the parent must step in and do so. Another task of parents is to step in and keep their children safe when they cannot keep themselves safe.

Richard and Theresa Baker I would listen to what my child has to tell me and establish the facts. Then I would try and explain why other children like to tease or bully and try and help my child deal with the kids who are acting in this way. If this didn't work for them, I would suggest seeing the children concerned or their parents and try and help them understand that teasing or bullying is not acceptable. When this happened to my kids at school (thankfully it wasn't often), I would make an appointment to see their class teacher or head teacher/principal and ask them to be aware of what was going on so they would, hopefully, keep an eye on things.

Kevin Johnson Tell them about 'Abdu'l-Bahá and how He handled things like this. If it gets really rough, talk to the school authorities and to the parents of the bully.

SCHOOL AND PEER-RELATED ISSUES

Donna Smith I would try to arrange a helpmate for my child, an older, calmer child who can intervene. My child did this for another and they became fast friends. Bullies threw stones at 'Abdu'l-Bahá when He was a child. As a parent, you need to pay attention and when such things come before you, act in a calm, purposeful way. Be a friend to your child. Each situation needs consultation, prayer and a different form of action.

John and Barbara Hartley We told our children to stand up for themselves and/or to ignore the ones who were doing it. We told them that if they did not react, then it would not be fun for the others to continue.

Andrew Adams I've told my son to try to avoid conflict. That is not always possible, particularly in the case of a bully. At school, he should tell his teacher or principal privately that he is being pestered. If, due to the lack of discipline and order in many schools, the bullying does not stop, I have counselled my son to defend himself.

If your child came home saying that he needed the 'right' kind of clothes or athletic shoes and was being laughed at for not having them, how would you deal with this?

Katayun Golshani Always, always, always acknowledge how hard it is to be laughed at and mocked by one's peers. Once you've acknowledged that and shared your sadness with the child, ask how he would like to handle this situation. Does he want to give in to this pressure and do as they want? Would he rather stand up and stick his ground? Or does he think that there is a wisdom in the way that they're looking at him, evaluating him and laughing at him? Does he truly think that his clothing or shoes need some reconsideration and need to be changed?

Bernice McKenzie I would tell them to save their money and buy them. Then I would give them chores to do to get the 'right' kind of clothes. The eldest always made her clothes and the youngest always had money, for some reason. We think she had the first penny I made.

Joe and Wilma Thompson We handled any request for name brand clothing by offering this solution. If it they wanted a brand of regular jeans, then we would pay the full amount. If they wanted designer jeans then they would have to pay. That left it for them to decide if the jeans were worth getting or not. This goes along with children assuming responsibility and consequences, which was at the core of our parenting.

Tanya Charles Clothes are both a 'need' and a 'want'. Within reason, I'm happy to let my kids have the clothes they like. I try to get their approval on the clothes I buy for them, usually by shopping with them.

Let's say we have finished shopping for jeans for this season. Now my daughter comes home and tells me she has to have a certain name brand or style. I would consider either offering to pay for part of the item or telling her I'd be happy to set up a time to take her to the mall so she could buy it – depending on my husband's and my evaluation of need, price and the social situation.

We just moved last summer and I did only part of the shopping for school clothes before school started. We had been living out of the country and in a completely different climate. I thought we all needed the opportunity to see what other kids were wearing before making all of our choices. The same may hold true with changing schools, say from grade school to middle school.

At this time I evaluate the kids' clothing needs with them a couple of times a year. Gradually, we plan to let our kids have some of the clothes budget each season and let them do the shopping for certain items. What better way to learn about sales and value than by making the decisions and bearing the consequences.

Finally, it is important to listen to the concerns our kids bring to us. Maybe the issue is really fitting in or being teased, not just clothes. I try to remind myself that things that sound unimportant to me as the parent were important to me when I was a teenager. The issues of their lives are different but not less important to them.

Simon Scott I have often explained how 'Abdu'l-Bahá lived the life of an 'Exemplar'. He did not wear the newest and finest clothes but gave them away to the poor. When one becomes addicted to status at an early age, it is merely the beginning of the worst kind of materialism.

John and Barbara Hartley We told them that they could have certain kinds of clothes or shoes if they were functional but not because everyone was wearing them. They did wear certain makes of athletic shoes because they were long-wearing and comfortable. They do not have a penchant for specific name brands. If they look good and feel good and are affordable, then they buy them.

Lucy Matthews We all have to deal with it. If you can afford it, to some extent, go along with it. There's nothing wrong with it in moderation. I don't think children are spoiled by the things they have but by feeling that they're the centre of the world, that they deserve them and they should automatically have them. The whole attitude of 'everything must revolve around me' is what must be avoided.

Beth Bishop This is difficult. I think you have to go along with it a bit but I drew the line at expensive trainers/sneakers for my daughter and bought baseball boots, which she set a fashion with. Not all children would be so confident.

Todd and Debbie McEwen We have given them a clothing allowance from the age of around 15. Before then, if they have wanted something particularly expensive, we would expect them to pay the extra cost over and above what we would consider the appropriate cost. In all cases we would consult with them about the real value of material things.

Margerie Gibson I'd say something along the lines of 'Grow up and get over it'. Our family policy has always been zero tolerance for stupid faddish things, from games like Pokemon to clothing. We all try to find the clothing we need at consignment shops, going to low-cost stores as a back-up and only going to a department store as a desperate last resort for something that we *must* have, that can't wait, such as the flower girl dress for my sister's wedding. Even then, we managed to find one on sale at 80 per cent off!

From what age (if at all) did you allow your teenager to attend 'teenage' parties?

George and Mary Burke Our children are not allowed to attend parties (if you mean parties in a school-peer sense). They accept this is an unsafe environment, typically unsupervised by adults and generally promiscuous. They don't participate.

Farzaneh Knight They are allowed to go but we have constantly reminded them that 'Abdu'l-Bahá is always present. We have been lucky to be able to have a high level of trust in our daughters. We know that they have thoroughly internalized their Bahá'í values. Ironically, because of this great freedom and no curfews, they were highly responsible and never abused that freedom. I have told them, 'I will not be with you all the time to watch over you but 'Abdu'l-Bahá *will*. If you do something that you are happy to have 'Abdu'l-Bahá see, go for it. Otherwise, don't do it.'

Julie Young The very first time that they attended co-ed parties was at middle/junior high school (ages 12 to 15). These were dances held at school. They were not allowed to go until they were in the eighth grade (ages 13 to 14). We manoeuvred our way in by volunteering to be the dance chaperones. We would always drop them off and pick them up. Our kids didn't go to many parties. If they did, they were parties with people that we knew very well. I can't remember a single Friday night that all three of our children were not with us.

SCHOOL AND PEER-RELATED ISSUES

Andrew Adams We allowed our children to attend afternoon school parties from the age of 12 and 13. They went to high school dances beginning at age 14. They go sometimes but not often. They know that their family is the centre of their social lives, not their friends.

Linda Bandari My children started to attend parties when they were 15. Most of the time it was with their Bahá'í friends at someone's home with parents at home. They were not allowed to attend parties at homes when the parents were not there. Most of the time they just hung out together – talking, eating and watching movies.

Joe and Wilma Thompson They had minimal exposure to parties until they were at college. They were always uncomfortable with the drinking and were often the 'designated driver' instead of being considered a 'prude'. We trusted them and they didn't disappoint us.

Kevin Johnson Sixteen. We had great alcohol-free swimming parties at our home, sometimes with up to a hundred kids. Many of these kids came to our firesides.

Melissa Taheri They were 16 and 18 when they first went to a party. When someone started tasting alcohol, the older one got his brother and they came home.

John and Barbara Hartley We did not restrict our teens when it came to attending parties.

Celia Stewart If I knew that there was going to be drinking or drugs, I wouldn't allow them to go at all. From the time they were in junior high (age 12), they were allowed to go to adult-supervised parties. They were not allowed to date or to go steady until they were 16.

Grace Simpson When she got to high school I let her go if I knew the friends. But she was very good at deciding between the parties she wanted to go to and the ones she knew she did not want to be at. If she knew there would be drugs and drinking, she didn't want to go.

Margerie Gibson She can attend a birthday party for friends that is supervised by responsible, *known* adults at any age! She is never allowed to attend an unsupervised party, just to 'party'.

6

Helping Your Child Understand the Sanctity of the Family

Is it more important to you that you be a parent to your child or a friend/buddy?

The members of a family all have duties and responsibilities towards one another and to the family as a whole, and these duties and responsibilities vary from member to member because of their natural relationships. The parents have the inescapable duty to educate their children – but not vice versa; the children have the duty to obey their parents – the parents do not obey the children . . .[1]

Donna Smith We need to be parents. Forget about being a buddy. When your child is an adult you will have a warm, loving, respectful friendship of trust, respect and love with each other. But while they are growing, they need you as a parent. They need someone who loves them enough to say no when appropriate. They need someone who will be their backbone as they learn and practise spiritual principles that will stand them in good stead all their life. They need parents to stand behind true principles. Parents are capable of maturity; children, until they are 15, are not. And maturity is needed for the learning and gradual application of principles.

George and Mary Burke We see our role of parents as primary. Our children have many friends but they only have us to serve as parents, so it is a role that only we can play.

Of course, in our role as parents, we play with our children and have many moments of fun, laughter and companionship. At times it can resemble a natural friendship between two people of very different ages. But our children have been well served by living within well-defined boundaries and it is our responsibility to create them and reinforce them. This clearly marked structure gives direction and organization to our children as well as the whole family.

Andrew Adams Parent. Though I like being a friendly parent.

Edyth Lewis When children are young, you are definitely a parent. As time passes, the relationship changes. By the time they are in their late teens, if you have worked at it, you become somewhere between a friend and a parent. The relationship may be a parent one minute, giving advice, and a friend the next, even asking advice from them.

Simon Scott I am not a friend or a buddy. This is some kind of concept that appeared in the 70s and, in my opinion, helped to reduce the respect for an older generation. I am a parent, a father, and love my daughters. I am not a peer. I come from a different generation that in some ways had values superior to those of today. As such, I do not try to emulate being something I am not – their peer.

Linda Bandari It was important to me to be there for my children in any role that I needed to play at the time. Sometimes I was a parent or authority, sometimes someone to console them or a shoulder to cry on, sometimes a listener or sounding board, sometimes an advisor, sometimes a friend to go to the movie with or to go shopping with, and so on.

Margerie Gibson Parent. I saw too many people close to me trying to be 'buddies' with their kids and everyone loses. Kids have plenty of 'buddies' in other kids. They only get one set of parents in this life and we have to do our job to allow them to have a good adulthood.

UNDERSTANDING THE SANCTITY OF THE FAMILY

Bernice McKenzie It is and was more important for me to be a friend to my children. They knew I was their mother and loved me for it but, as they both said, it was so important to be loved unconditionally. They knew that no matter what happened in their lives, they could come to me and talk about it.

Barbara Hartley As a mother, it was important to me to be a parent to the children because I felt they had enough buddies but only one mother.

Julie Young It is far more important to us that we be parents to our children. We don't want to be a friend or buddy. I don't believe that you can be a buddy to adult children. The child can have only one mother and father.

Katayun Golshani My children can have many friends but they can only have one mother. I'll always remain their parent. As my children get older, the dynamics change. We then associate as friends. As they grow and have their own children, my role of friend becomes far more needed and appropriate. My role becomes one of an older, wiser friend – one who listens, affirms and empathizes. So as children get older, the parenting role changes.

What did you do when siblings fought?

Lucy Matthews My brother and I fought. My mother told us that we must treat each other like princes and princesses. It didn't stop us fighting. My mother told us to sit down in separate places and read a book. Siblings fight. If things got too out of hand, she'd send us to do our homework. If we didn't have homework, we had to sit down, get quiet and read a book for ten minutes or so. My mother didn't really scold us. She tried to get us to respect each other. She was calm.

Michelle Sharpe We had time-out for both of them. We then had them discuss and come up with solutions. Sometimes, if the solutions were worked out quickly, we did not have punishments. If they continued, they would be deprived of TV or visiting a friend.

Farzaneh Knight They fought a lot. We got them separate bedrooms. The family conferences helped. With time and maturity they became very close friends. They are now inseparable. They are always phoning and emailing one another.

Katayun Golshani There's a wonderful book called *Siblings Without Rivalry* by the same authors (Adele Faber and Elaine Mazlish) who wrote *How to Talk So Kids Will Listen and Listen So Kids Will Talk*. Parents need to become aware that when siblings fight, it does not happen without some kind of a prelude. It usually has a start and then it crescendos. They could be sitting and playing in the kitchen, for example. Then one of them starts insulting the other and calling him names. Then they start arguing back and forth. The parents need to be aware and do something to divert that. They need to have zero tolerance for calling each other names, saying bad words and not cooperating with each other. The rule should be, 'I'd rather you enjoy each other's company, work with each other, help each other and have fun together. If you do so, you can have everything you want.' God tells His servants that when we are in unity it is life and when we are in disunity it is death. So you tell them that as long as they are in unity with each other, they can have the toy and play together. Once they start fighting, the toy will be taken away. You don't need to sit there and make a judgement as to whose fault it is and who was good or bad. Just because they're in disunity, they will lose the privilege and opportunity of having the toy. The children will soon get the message that fighting won't get them anywhere.

John and Barbara Hartley When they were of pre-school age, I went into the bathroom with a good book and locked the door. They usually stopped when they no longer had an audience. Other times I would separate them or send them to their respective rooms.

Linda Bandari My children were very close in age and very competitive. They often would 'push each other's buttons' and get into a fight. They tried to get me to take sides. When they got out of control I would make them go to their own rooms until they cooled down. Later we would talk about what had happened. They would usually admit to purposely trying to bug the other over something trivial. The problem lessened as they got older.

Melissa Taheri Unfortunately I wasn't always consistent. I tried to take action if the situation was very unfair to one or if one was being hurt. Things seemed to resolve themselves better if I didn't interfere.

Joe and Wilma Thompson That didn't happen often but when it did we would try and let them resolve it through consulting. They often say they were born consulting! Their fights were usually due to normal sibling relationships but they often needed to 'clear the air'.

Todd and Debbie McEwen We have told them both off (not just the perpetrator – unless it was clearly one-sided) and told them to sort out their differences together properly. This has now ceased to be a problem.

What should be done about sibling rivalry?

Donna Smith We used to separate them for a time if they were disagreeing. We would pay attention if we heard wrangling but we insisted that they work it out between themselves and they turned to us only as a higher court when absolutely necessary. Oftentimes we would talk about the rivalry at family consultation when things were calm and would try to listen to the different needs. We would make them apologize to each other and shake hands (we have three boys). We tried to spend some time with each child alone and would do something special with each of them – go to a ball game or the store or take a walk, for instance. All three boys are close in spirit and write emails back and forth nowadays and get together as often as possible, even though they each live thousands of miles apart.

Donald Pope Begin by showing a good example of how to get along and how to handle differences as they occur.

Maintain parental unity. Avoid letting children play one parent against another. Emphasize the need for family unity and encourage the children to support one another.

If the children start to squabble, both get time-out and are asked after the time-out if they are ready to play together peacefully or what they can do if they can't.

Praise each child for the excellence you see in them and never compare them. Only compare them with themselves. Rejoice in any gain.

Accept no backbiting or gossip from anyone!

With all you do, be aware that some sibling rivalry is natural. How you respond to it is what will make the difference.

Michelle Sharpe This was one of the most difficult things to deal with. We talked a lot and encouraged them to do things together.

Whenever their friends come over, it's good to be sure to include the sibling. Having a friend for one sibling visit causes a lot of jealousy and resentment if the other sibling is left out.

Edyth Lewis It is inevitable that the oldest child, merely by dint of being two or more years older than his siblings, will have abilities that the others don't have. The parents' expectations of a two year old are quite different from their expectations of a six year old. If a toddler draws on the wall then the parents get a bucket of water and wash the drawing off. If a four year old draws on the wall then the parents try to explain why it is not a good thing. A six year old could be disciplined by his parents for drawing on an inappropriate surface. However, the six year old may not appreciate why he gets into trouble when his younger siblings do not and may try to use the discipline that is appropriate for his own age group on his younger brother or sister when he sees them doing something that he is not allowed to do. It was only when talking to my eldest son when he was in his twenties that I realized that this had been the case in our family. Had I realized that he was trying to make his brother and sister behave 'better', then I think I would not have been so hard on him or would at least have worked through the real problem rather than my perception that he was either jealous of them or attention-seeking for himself.

With a two and a half year age gap between our sons it was inevitable that the older one would be able to do things that the younger one would not. The older one was very good at teaching himself. You only had to give him an instruction book and he had mastered whatever it was that he was trying to learn. We decided that when the younger one wanted to learn the guitar it was important that his older brother did not touch it, just so that there was something about which the younger one would not have to compete with his brother.

Todd and Debbie McEwen We have always encouraged them to be individuals and praised them for what they are good at, stressing that they have talents in different areas. We have also treated them all as equally as we can.

Linda Bandari I can't say that I ever resolved sibling rivalry. I can say that I kept it to a tolerable level. Since my children were close in age they were very competitive about most things. I am not sure that was all bad. It made them work harder and strive to do better than they might have otherwise.

Tom and Andrea Edwards We tried to make sure that they were getting enough attention from us.

Melissa Taheri I don't think that sibling rivalry has been resolved totally yet. We've taken time with each child alone all their lives and have tried to make each child feel important to us. Each child is expected to support the other. The older one has attended more of his brother's basketball and soccer games than he probably wanted to and the younger one has gone to more orchestra concerts than he would have liked to attend. We have tried to stress that we are a family and members support each other. They still don't always get along but their friendship seems to be getting stronger as they grow older.

How did you help your child learn the principle of consultation?

Irene Dominguez We began consulting with our children from the time they were three or four years old. We would call everyone to the room and tell them the topic of consultation. We would then ask everyone for their opinion. This is a principle that they have understood greatly. They often seek consultation themselves.

Edyth Lewis Even when they were small we tried to involve the children in decision-making appropriate to their age in an informal way. We tried having formal family meetings but these never worked very well. The family always ate dinner together around the table and this was often the forum for bringing up subjects for consultation. The other occasion was late at night. This was often when someone had an issue that he could not resolve by himself. These were always the best consultations. They took half the night but usually had some resolution to them.

Linda Bandari We involved our children in consultation when they were school age. We usually had family consultation every one to two weeks depending on what there was to consult about. It was also a good time to talk about Bahá'í virtues and how we could put them into practice. We consulted about a variety of subjects that affected our children. For example, there were some older children on the school bus with our children. Some of the older children behaved inappropriately so we consulted on what were the best ways for our children to deal with the situation.

Donna Smith I was rigid about consultation when we first became

UNDERSTANDING THE SANCTITY OF THE FAMILY

Bahá'ís. We would sit down every Friday evening. Someone would be secretary, someone chair and we would discuss. Discussions were mainly focused on their wants and complaints when they were little. After consultation, which was not really a bed of roses, we would do something fun as a family. They gradually learned that consultation was far more effective than whining or manipulative behaviour. By the time we had our third child, consultation had become a much looser and ingrained habit that they simply accepted. We would have an easy Bahá'í book on the table. Each night at supper one of us would read a short quotation from it and then strive to talk about it. At least they were being constantly educated in the writings that way.

Once our dishwasher broke down. We discovered that more real consultation got done when one parent and one child were washing the dishes together. Thoughts about the day just automatically came up. I don't think the way you do it is at all important. Looking back, I would just say that one should make an effort to consult about everything that is needed and then everyone – adults included – learn that consultation is the best way of coping with life.

Todd and Debbie McEwen We have not generally held meetings specifically for family consultation. However, whenever the need arises, we will consult with them on an individual or family basis and to a greater degree as their maturity increases. Consultation about anything is more a way of life than a specific activity taught at a particular time. It starts, in a limited way, as soon as they start to communicate.

Lucy Matthews When I was growing up consultation just happened naturally in my family. When I was unhappy about something at school, mother sat down with me and said, 'Let's talk about it.' Then she talked about learning how to cope with problems using the 'Remover of Difficulties'.

I remember when I was crying over not being able to do my homework when I was in the seventh grade. My mother listened and said, 'Come on, let's go for a drive.' She took me in the car. I have no memory of what she said. But I know that she must have been talking about laying your problems in God's hands, backing off and saying the 'Remover of Difficulties'. What she said was deeply spiritual. I was almost 12 years old and that was the day that I became a Bahá'í. I had the experience of ecstasy. I have no desire to experience that again in this world. That's for the next world. If you've had it, you've had it. You don't need to have it over and over again. My mother talked to me. I was very free. She was a listening ear. I could say whatever I felt. I don't remember ever sitting down and saying, 'Now let's consult about this.' It was simply very casual. It was consultation but I wasn't aware of it. A family isn't a democracy. The parents have to have control. But the children should be free to give their input and know that it will be taken seriously.

Margerie Gibson Angus and I consult on everything from what colour to paint the kitchen to what curriculum we should choose for Kendra's maths (Kendra is home-schooled). She has seen consultation in action all her life. We have family consultation for planning our activities, working on our relationships and for resolving disputes or tensions. We ask her for her input and opinions as we would anyone else.

Farzaneh Knight We have had family conferences from a very early age. We start with prayers. The person who feels the most hurt or has the most concerns gets to talk first. All have to listen quietly. Interrupting is strictly forbidden. Then the next person can speak. We then have an open discussion. There are tears, hugs, laughter and appreciations. And the family has upped its unity and strength one more notch.

How can we teach our kids to be selective and successful when choosing a spouse?

Melissa Taheri This is an ongoing process and I think it begins when the parent helps the child choose friends by looking at the qualities and characters of his acquaintances. We've talked about marriage and dating and that marriage needs shared values, goals and interests, not just physical attraction. Both understand the law of consent of parents and I think that will make them choose more carefully.

Todd and Debbie McEwen We have taught them what the Bahá'í writings say about selecting a spouse, particularly that they should 'become thoroughly acquainted with the character of the other'.[2] Also, when the time comes, we will make sure that we consider things very carefully before giving permission to marry.

Simon Scott I have served on local spiritual assemblies for 27 years. During that time I have sat in on 22 Bahá'í divorces. The couples have been of various national backgrounds – in fact, the background of the couples made little difference. The tears that I have seen, complaints that I have heard, the loss of individuals who leave the Faith and take their children with them after a divorce, all have led me to my current opinion that something is wrong with our selection process for potential spouses. None of the 44 individuals that I dealt with seemed to be an intrinsically bad person. It is my opinion that these couples were mismatched in any number of ways.

'Abdu'l-Bahá says that we should become fully acquainted with the character of an individual we are considering marrying. Thus far it seems that most people are using the same criteria as they did in the past – love, physical attractiveness and so on. If that is true, why is it that so many people choose marriage partners that they later feel aversion towards? I would suggest that not only is love sometimes 'blind', sometimes it is also dumb. Parents should be impartial evaluators of their child's choice of spouse. The parents know their child's true character. At the same time, the parents are not swayed by the romantic inclinations of their child. As such they should be able to help identify common ground and sources of differences between the potential marriage partners that the couple may not be objective or mature enough to recognize.

I have every intention of ascertaining the character, values and personality 'fit' of any potential suitors to my daughters, and as I have told members of my community, I won't hesitate to refuse parental permission if I sense the marriage would be 'wrong' in any way and would lead to the emotional hurt, scarring and financial loss that I have seen in so many Bahá'í divorces.

There is a great book called *The Chosen Highway* by Lady Blomfield describing her visits and talks with 'Abdu'l-Bahá in the early 20th century. She describes two cases of Bahá'ís seeking approval for a divorce from 'Abdu'l-Bahá. In one case 'Abdu'l-Bahá granted a divorce, in the other He did not. Lady Blomfield was told by 'Abdu'l-Bahá that divorce was abhorrent to Bahá'u'lláh and that the solution to problems within marriage was not to make divorce easier to obtain but to make marriage more difficult. Finally, if one of my children gave me an ultimatum, then somehow they missed the lesson on the requirement for parental permission and respect for the parents. My purpose is not to make my child unhappy but in a case where I think for whatever reason that the marriage is 'wrong', then I am going to prevent her from enduring the pain of divorce. I am willing to endure the anger of my child at being prevented from marrying poorly if it means that she will not suffer the pain and hurt that I have seen in the 22 Bahá'í divorces I have witnessed.

As a parting suggestion, I recommend that Bahá'ís find and study Amatu'l-Bahá Rúḥíyyih Khánum's *Prescription for Living* as it gives some interesting insights on marriage that is neither eastern nor western in design or intent.

Bernice McKenzie Try and have a good marriage. Talk about what's important in marriage. I always asked my daughters, 'What are the qualities you will bring to the marriage?'

Farzaneh Knight If the children have internalized the right values, they will be drawn to good partners. But we do tell our children always to think of the spouse as a parent of their future children. Would they want to have a child with this person? Will their child be proud to have such a person as their parent? Will this person love Bahá'u'lláh as much as they do? Will he be as active as she is or will he be jealous of the Faith and hamper her activities? This would be unbearable.

John and Barbara Hartley We can ask them to look at how that person treats others and see if that's the way they want to be treated. We can ask them what they are looking for in a spouse. We can suggest that they spend time together on projects with others so they can judge whether they would be compatible.

Edyth Lewis A number of years ago some of our peers got together to discuss our responsibilities for giving permission for our children to get married. We realized that we should have started this process at the time that the children were very young.

My husband and I and another friend ran a seminar for youth on marriage and I have also been involved in a training programme that was put together by the European Task Force for the Family on choosing a partner, married life and child rearing.

I told my own children to look very closely at the parents of their intended – how the parents related to each other and what their assumptions were. These are likely to be the values that their intended has picked up. If the family resolves issues by shouting at each other then it is likely that this will be brought into their marriage and they need to be prepared for it or find another partner. They also need to look at how the parents divide responsibilities. If, for instance, it is the father of the girl's family who is in charge of finances and the mother of the boy's family then they could be in trouble as both will think that the other partner should look after financial matters. These issues and assumptions will need special discussion and consideration.

Richard and Theresa Baker I think that general talking and discussion about these matters helps as the children are growing up. They also observe their parents' generation and how they have handled marriages. Obviously, it is a great help to them to have a stable family unit where their own parents have a successful marriage.

Our son got married (just before his 28th birthday) two years ago to a lovely Irish Baháʼí he met at a Baháʼí youth gathering in the UK. I can honestly say that I couldn't have selected a better wife for him had I done the choosing myself!

Paul Oliver Train them from the beginning as virtuous human beings. What I have told my daughter is that when you think that he is 'the one', look at him through my eyes because I will have veto power.

Lucy Matthews This is a hard one. Every couple is different. Everyone is putting up a front when dating. You're not really getting to know the person. Go do something worthwhile. Do some teaching or service together. This is how you'll learn the character of the other person. You have to do more than have fun when selecting a mate.

What would you do if you felt pressured to give consent for your child's marriage but had doubts?

In many cases of breach of marriage laws the believers apparently look upon the law requiring consent of parents before marriage as a mere administrative regulation, and do not seem to realize that this is a law of great importance affecting the very foundations of human society. Moreover, they seem not to appreciate that in the Baháʼí Faith the spiritual and administrative aspects are complementary and that the social laws of the Faith are as binding as the purely spiritual ones.[3]

It is perfectly true that Baháʼu'lláh's statement that the consent of all living parents is required for marriage places a grave responsibility on each parent. When the parents are Baháʼís they should, of course, act objectively in withholding or granting their approval.

UNDERSTANDING THE SANCTITY OF THE FAMILY

They cannot evade this responsibility by merely acquiescing in their child's wish, nor should they be swayed by prejudice; but, whether they be Bahá'í or non-Bahá'í, the parents' decision is binding, whatever the reason that may have motivated it. Children must recognize and understand that this act of consenting is the duty of a parent. They must have respect in their hearts for those who have given them life, and whose good pleasure they must at all times strive to win.[4]

Donald Pope I take the law of consent very seriously! The parents must exercise the right of sober second thought on the decisions of the young. They stand before God for their decision, support or no support. The purpose of the law is unity.

If you feel pressured but have doubts, voice your doubts and then offer a way that your doubts can be laid to rest. Say, 'I would have to see your girlfriend before I can be sure that I can trust her.' Make it possible for the couple to demonstrate what you need to see.

Once parents give consent, they assume a spiritual obligation to fully welcome the new person and their extended family into their own family!

Andrew Adams This is our sacred obligation. We must fulfil it. I plan to exercise this duty with the utmost care and concern. I will not give consent if I have doubts.

Julie Young This is something that I am very scared about. I take the law of parental consent very seriously. I would never give in if I had any doubts.

Michelle Sharpe I take it very seriously. The law of consent is divine guidance that Bahá'u'lláh has given us. The family is the foundation. This law is a wonderful way to be involved in the selection of a spouse.

It must be difficult if the parents do not approve for whatever reason. However, it is for the best.

If I felt pressured to give consent, but had doubts, it would hurt greatly. I would not feel good about being pressured. It would be far better to discuss the doubts now instead of pretending and having regrets later on.

Linda Bandari When I got married I was not a Bahá'í but my husband was. He mentioned to me that he wanted to get consent from our parents. I thought that it was a good idea, as I wanted my parents' approval anyway. When our children came to us for consent, I felt comfortable with their choices. They both married into very wonderful Bahá'í families. We feel truly blessed. If that had not been the case, then I would have voiced my concerns and had a serious discussion about my reservations. If they could give me logical reasons as to why these concerns were unfounded or how they could be worked out, then I would give my consent.

Margerie Gibson I take the law of parental consent *very* seriously! My parents died when I was quite young, so I had to depend on my potential mates' parents to use good judgement. The first set of parents gave consent without fully or seriously considering the consent issue. That marriage was a disaster, ending in divorce after five years. There followed two other attempts to marry, both times we were refused consent by the parents of my boyfriends. Hindsight has allowed me to be grateful to those parents for refusing their consent! I can't imagine having been happy in a relationship with either of those men. Finally, I received thoughtful consent from the parents of my beloved husband and deeply felt the difference between being consciously welcomed into a loving family versus the indifference displayed by my first husband's family. I would never give consent if I had any doubts.

If my child gave us an ultimatum, it would demonstrate even more fully that my child was too immature to marry!

7

Creating a Home Environment Conducive to Material and Spiritual Welfare

Did either one of you stay home to be a full-time parent when the children were young?

... O maid-servants of the Merciful! It is incumbent upon you to train the children from their earliest babyhood! It is incumbent upon you to beautify their morals! It is incumbent upon you to attend to them under all aspects and circumstances, inasmuch as God – glorified and exalted is He! – hath ordained mothers to be the primary trainers of children and infants. This is a great and important affair and a high and exalted position, and it is not allowable to slacken therein at all![1]

With regard to your question whether mothers should work outside the home, it is helpful to consider the matter from the pespective of the concept of a Bahá'í family. This concept is based on the principle that the man has primary responsibility for the financial support of the family, and the woman is the chief and primary educator of the children. This by no means implies that these functions are inflexibly fixed and cannot be changed and adjusted to suit particular family situations, nor does it mean that the place of the woman is confined to the home. Rather, while primary responsibility is assigned, it is anticipated that fathers would play a significant role in the education of the children and women could also be breadwinners. As you rightly indicated, 'Abdu'l-Bahá encouraged women to 'participate fully and equally in the affairs of the world'.[2]

Richard and Theresa Baker As mother, I stayed home full time. Before my first child was born I thought of returning to work but from the moment my son arrived, I no longer wanted to leave him and go out to work. I was fortunate in living overseas in that I did not have to work.

When we returned to live in the UK (the children were then aged 13 and 10) I used to work part time but from home. Some of the most precious talks I had with the children were when they came home from school and could talk over the day's activities with me and discuss any problems they might have. As parents, we always made time to listen to our children.

We both loved every moment of being parents to our young children and every moment of being a parent to them as they grew up. Now that they are young adults and have left home, we miss them! We feel that it was very important for them to have had a full-time parent (mother) at home for them. I was able to give them quality time all the time and we have no doubt in our minds that it has benefited them all the way.

Grace Simpson I was a single parent when she was born and could only take off seven months. But it was a wonderful time to spend with her. It is so important to stay home with your children but to be a part of their lives and do things together – not just to clean house and take care of them but to really help deepen them and train them.

Edyth Lewis I was a full-time mother from before my eldest child was born and until my youngest child went to school. After that, I worked from home for a while and then took part-time jobs that would allow me to be at home during the school holidays. I would not have done any of this differently. It did mean that we had to make sacrifices and that we were not as rich as we would have been had I gone out to work.

CREATING A CONDUCIVE HOME ENVIRONMENT

Michelle Sharpe I stayed home and worked from home part time with our second child. I did this for the first four years. This is very important to us as it provides quality care and education in the early years. We always left the house together and one of us was there to pick them up from school.

Irene Dominguez From the time we got married, we decided that I would stay home for at least the first two years of the children's lives. It really made a difference in their behaviour. We felt better as parents because we could teach them good manners, talk about God and share chores. Since I am a Montessori teacher, they then went with me to pre-school, even though I was not able to be with them all the time.

Celia Stewart My oldest child was in daycare but I was a stay-at-home mom with the other three children. I think it is best for the children and best for the mother. I stayed at home with the kids when they were little and went on to have a career when they were older.

Angela Brown This must be a matter of consultation among Bahá'í couples, as the husband is still the one charged with primary responsibilities for the welfare of the family while the wife is primarily responsible for the care and training of the children.

I have been in three situations – staying at home to raise children, a single mother and a married working mother.

In the first situation, I raised all three of my daughters until the third began first grade (age 6). During that time I began an art school in my basement, including a small studio for my children, and took care of other's children. This provided a little income and allowed me to be with my children during these formative years. After the divorce from my first husband, I returned to college and began working. I completed my higher degrees and took my children to a pioneering post in Malaysia. We went travel teaching on a shoestring fellowship budget.

I remarried 18 years ago. We had our son. By then I was in my career as a college faculty, so we arranged for me to be home during the day and to take a teaching job at night during the first few years. We then asked an elderly Baháʼí to care for our son in the home. When he was three and a half we sought out good daycare near the college where I taught. This was not so easy to find. Many daycares are shallow in their expectations and in their genuine love for children. Our son was frightened and terrified to go to those. We prayed and found one which was not so rich as the others in appearance but in which a great deal of real character training and concern for each child was apparent. Our son loved this centre and I became involved in working with it and with its teachers.

So I would say that being home is the best, but when not possible, it is essential to pray for guidance in finding daycare that has a staff of warm, loving people with good character and with a philosophy, discipline and programme that matches up as closely with the Baháʼí standards as possible.

Melissa Taheri No, I have always worked part time because it would be hard to get back into community health nursing if I left. I knew I could support our family if the need arose. When my husband visited his parents in Iran for the first time in years (the boys were 10 and 12), he felt he could go because I could take care of the boys if he were not able to come back. I worked two to three days a week and took a three-month maternity leave with each. I have mixed feelings now about having worked but I had a good situation. I was able to nurse each child until the child was ready to stop and I was there if the boys were sick or had a programme at school. Violin lessons at school were on my lunch break and I volunteered at school. The boys knew I would help with activities on my days off, and so, if a driver or something else were needed, they would volunteer me without asking me. My job has always been on weekdays; I think I would have felt differently if I had had to work on weekends when they were not in school.

Nina Sadaghiyan I stayed home for the first seven years with our oldest and for five years with the youngest. It is very important for the child to know that he is safe and that his parents are there for him at all times. If there was one thing that I would change, it would be to being more patient.

Andrew Adams Angie stayed home with Mary and Trevor until Trevor turned four. We believe strongly in spending as much time with our kids as possible. We feel the same way now that they are adults as we did then.

Donna Smith I was fortunate in being able to stay home with our children. I did do some part-time nursing but I was always really a stay-at-home mom. I feel grateful that was granted to us and we could actually do it. We lived simply. We were probably always in debt but it was an investment in their souls which we were never sorry about. The house is empty of our children now and I work all the time. Believe me, there are plenty of years for women to work and you bring a wealth of experience to the workplace if you have been a stay-at-home mom. Basically, you just don't know you have it. Parenting is the most difficult job in the world. Anything else is a piece of cake if you have been a stay-at-home mom. I wouldn't change a single thing.

What are your feelings about daycare?

> With reference to the question of the training of children: given the emphasis placed by Bahá'u'lláh and 'Abdu'l-Bahá on the necessity for the parents to train their children while still in their tender age, it would seem preferable that they should receive their first training at home at the hand of their mother, rather than be sent to a nursery. Should circumstances, however, compel a Bahá'í mother to adopt the latter course there can be no objection.[3]

Donald Pope If you are not willing to invest five years where at least one parent's primary concern is raising the next generation, avoid having children. As a clinical child psychologist, I saw many children and they all had problems. Some of their problems were due to the presence of their parents. Many were due to the emotional and other sorts of absence of their parents. A child's character is pretty well set by the age of seven. Invest heavily in your children during those years and they, you and humanity will reap a lifetime worth of rewards.

With some exceptions, daycare is the worst concept that the West has convinced parents that they cannot live without. It will never be a substitute for real family or extended family. When I was in training there was concern about the impact that the kibbutz daycare centres were having on children in Israel. Today, the problems they are having are multiplied ten-fold on the average child in North America. With that said, there are a few excellent ones out there, perhaps one in a hundred.

Grace Simpson I had to put her in daycare and she enjoyed it. If I could have stayed home, it would have been better.

John and Barbara Hartley We were fortunate for we could afford to have mother home for the first five years of each child's life, therefore she positively influenced the boys on a daily basis. It is much more difficult today for one of the parents to stay home because of the expense involved in raising children. If a family is willing to sacrifice some of the material things, then having a parent stay home with the children is still possible, even now. Having a parent at home might prevent the child from experiencing the normal interaction with his peers. We overcame this by being involved in a community playgroup. The playgroup was filled with babies, toddlers and pre-schoolers. It had many interactive activities.

Daycares are acceptable if they meet some basic criteria. A well-trained and professional staff is critical. A small ratio of daycare worker to children to insure each child gets the necessary attention, as well as a safe and clean facility is also necessary. A comprehensive, stimulating and interactive programme is necessary. Ideally, children should be in daycare no sooner than after they walk and have some capacity to talk.

CREATING A CONDUCIVE HOME ENVIRONMENT

Paul Oliver I think daycare should be a decision only for a single parent who has no other support.

Irene Dominguez We don't like daycare. That's why I stayed home with our children for their first two years. They then went with me to the Montessori pre-school where I taught.

Celia Stewart I think daily daycare should be a last resort. I have worked in daycare and even the best daycares aren't able to give children the unconditional love of a parent or grandparent. Having a child in daycare for a 'mother's day out' is good, so that a child learns that a parent leaves and comes back.

Phoebe Untekar I am not in favour of full-time daycare, although I realize that in many cases there is no other choice. I think that pre-school a few times a week can be a great experience for a child however.

Linda Paulson Through circumstances, all my children were in daycare at one time or another. The larger daycares such as a Montessori school have their place in teaching children certain skills such as learning and physical skills but they are also breeders of germs. Eventually I took my children out of daycare facilities and put them with a private babysitter at her home because there were fewer children, therefore they were less likely to become sick.

Also, I believe in 'coffee breaks' for parents. Whoever is home taking care of the children needs an occasional break from the kids, so putting them with a babysitter for a few hours two or three days a week does no harm and gives the children opportunities to develop social skills with other children.

Margerie Gibson I think daycare is a last resort in certain cases – if a parent becomes widowed or disabled and a mother has to return to work and there are no relatives or close friends who can care for the child. I don't think children in most families should be cared for anyone but their parents, at any age.

Kevin Johnson Many have to resort to daycare because of economic necessity. It is best if the mother stays home until the children start school.

Beth Bishop I am not in favour unless one really needs the money. By putting the child in daycare, the parent misses out on so much, as well as have other people shaping the child's mind. However, once they are three they need to go somewhere for two mornings a week or so. This can be built up to more at the age of four. Ours went to the village playgroup for two mornings at the age of two and a half and also to a nursery school three mornings a week from the age of four or so.

Michelle Sharpe I feel that daycare should not be an option in the early years as these are the years to provide spiritual education. We have not understood the importance of parents raising their children. We have lost our way, thinking that we must have two salaries. We have embraced the material world to the detriment of our children. Our children do not benefit from material things. The children of Bahá are blessed that they are in the forefront of this Faith. However, even Bahá'ís are lost materially too. When we look at the non-Bahá'í world, we see how the children and youth are so angry and so misplaced. They feel abandoned and unloved. We must now understand that our spiritual needs come first. When we do this for our children they will thank us later. We all know kids that grew up with material affluence. I am now speaking of very wealthy families. When we listen to these children, oftentimes they literally 'hate' their parents and have little love. The parents were too busy maintaining their wealth and lost their children through drugs, etc.

What is your opinion about babysitters?

Andrew Adams Once in a while we would hire a babysitter. Usually we enjoyed doing things together as a family of four, rather

CREATING A CONDUCIVE HOME ENVIRONMENT

than the two of us (parents) going somewhere by ourselves. Seeing a movie was not as interesting or fun as being home with our kids.

Linda Paulson Choose your babysitters wisely. They should be responsible, conscientious and they should genuinely like children. We've had teenage babysitters as well as older babysitters. The teenagers were told that if something went wrong, they were to call their own parents immediately to come over and then to get hold of us. The older babysitters knew first aid, were resourceful and could handle almost any problem that came up.

My first child was what is called a 'strong willed child'. She was born with strong opinions and disposition. When she was a baby, she was well-mannered as long as she could see me. About three times a week, I would go to the gym for about an hour and a half with a friend. My friend's teenage daughter babysat for me. My friend was a Bahá'í but her daughter was still undecided. When I would get ready to leave, my baby would start to cry and fuss a lot. The only way to quiet her down when she got like this was to read the Tablet of Aḥmad twice. (Yes, twice – once would not do it. This is how stubborn this child was.) The teenager was left with an open prayer book turned to the Tablet of Aḥmad with instructions to read this prayer twice and the baby would quiet down. The first time we left her with the screaming baby and prayer book, she gave me a look of 'how can you do this to me?' Apparently she read the Tablet twice and the baby quieted down so she could play with her. After that, she became accustomed to reading this prayer. Eventually, the teenager signed her declaration card.

Margerie Gibson No. The only childcare I ever used was a close friend or a family member.

Donald Pope An old Chinese saying goes, 'A child is a blank page upon which everyone writes'. The best way to serve God is to raise the children. Babysitters ought to be a last resort. Their character ought to meet or exceed your own. You must trust the sitter, not only to be responsible but also to be a good influence on the child, as well as fun. If you can't find that, then cancel your plans or make it a family affair.

Edyth Lewis When they were young the children were sometimes left in the evening with people they knew. As they grew up, I was part of a babysitting circle and they were looked after by people they didn't know. They didn't seem to object to this. They usually had gone to bed by the time the babysitter arrived.

Grace Simpson I very rarely left her with babysitters. My experience with young babysitters was not good. I had a wonderful neighbour who adored her and took good care of her when I needed a sitter.

Nina Sadaghiyan We didn't leave our children with babysitters.

Celia Stewart We left our kids with babysitters occasionally. This was usually someone we knew very well. We would take that time to go on a 'date' so that we could reconnect and keep the adult portion of our marriage alive.

Richard and Theresa Baker Yes, we would from time to time leave our children with babysitters. When the children were young they didn't like it. As they got a bit older, they became more resigned to it. Obviously there are times when parents have to go out and leave their children but we didn't do it a great deal and always looked forward to getting home and seeing them again!

Michelle Sharpe This is such a difficult one to answer. I feel that children should be raised by their parents until the age of five. Babysitters should be in a supporting role and not in a parenting role. Looking back now, I would do it differently. Nancy had a babysitter at nine months. I stayed home for Joseph.

Angela Brown I feel strongly that anyone who is going to be with our children, for either a short or extended period of time, should

CREATING A CONDUCIVE HOME ENVIRONMENT

be individuals with good character who are reliable and trustworthy, as well as kind, loving and competent. These situations work best when parents spend time getting to know the individuals concerned and training them to carry out the 'programme' which the parents feel works best in their family for their children. So in this sense the individual can be seen as a member of the family, an older sibling, an aunt or uncle, or a grandparent, who is implementing what has already been planned, rather than just hanging out with the children in a completely serendipitous fashion.

In his book, *Mothers, Fathers, and Children*, the Hand of the Cause of God Mr Furutan makes a point that during the brief period of childhood, every hour and minute can be seen as a teachable moment, if we are to take advantage of the capacities of children to learn. We must also recognize their playful and affectionate natures. Time can be planned wherein children are enjoying some activity which involves active play, storytelling and quiet, as well as some delicious and nutritious food. Therefore when an individual is with the child, it should be planned as a delightful, safe experience for all but also one in which there is at least a potential for learning. I would then definitely maintain as close contact as possible with the child and individual caring for the child to see how things are going, whether some adjustment in plans needs to be made, whether a quarrel has arisen or whether there has been an accident.

Joe and Wilma Thompson Absolutely *vital*! The couple needs to be strengthened. Your relationship should not be tabled just because you have children. Often you can 'swap' this with another mother if finances are a consideration. But by all means, have some time for yourself and your spouse!

Irene Dominguez We never left our children with babysitters. We always managed to take them to even the most difficult of places. They have learned to suffer from the time they were young. Hardship has made them stronger and has taught them to understand the feelings of others, as well as the ways that others live. We took our oldest daughter with us on a teaching trip from the time she was four months old. I loved carrying them with me in a baby carrier. They were always with us.

When your children were babies, how would you react to nighttime waking?

John and Barbara Hartley Our oldest child was eagerly awaited and joyously received. We held him a lot and rocked him to sleep. He was two and a half years old before he would fall asleep on his own. On the advice of our doctor, we let him cry himself to sleep to break him of the habit of having to rock him. It took about five days. We would walk around the house, play the stereo to avoid picking him up during this time.

We let our second child cry himself to sleep if he was fed and dry. It is interesting to note that Peter, our firstborn, did not have a security blanket, but Charles, our second, did. Peter is very dependent on relationships and approval. Charles is more independent and better trusts his own ideas.

Donna Smith I did both. I comforted them at times and at other times, I let them cry it out. It is a 'fly by the seat of your pants' type of thing. Each child is so unique. Some you let them cry because they are just trying to manipulate you. Others truly need you to comfort and care for them. This advice is probably not all that helpful but you have to use the common sense God gave you to handle each child differently. One of my children was so sensitive, I just had to lift my eyebrow and he felt it. Another was impervious to any and all warnings and needed a very firm hand. A firm hand with the other child would have crushed his spirit.

Paul Oliver We usually comforted them until a pattern arose. Then we needed to let them cry it out for our own sanity. It worked. Hopefully it did not traumatize them for life.

CREATING A CONDUCIVE HOME ENVIRONMENT

Angela Brown Perhaps the main thing to remember is that this period of parenting is very brief in the span of the parenting journey! Most of the issues facing us are apt to cause a great deal of mental anguish, whereas restless children usually cause sleep deprivation and some concerns.

Out of the four children I have raised, two had colic. During the first four months, they screamed in pain for many nights, requiring my husband and me to walk the floor. We would rock them, worry, pray and sing a bit more than usual. Amazingly, it passed and that test was over!

Another child had a hard time going to sleep until midnight (a pattern which has continued in her adult years). She would constantly call for me, complaining of ghosts and goblins in her room, of sadness or anything to get me to spend a few hours with her comforting her. Perhaps I should have given her the option of getting up, turning on the light and reading until she felt sleepy. I usually had prayers and stories with the children but this was a long extension of that special time with all of the children.

I don't agree that children should be left to cry alone. That same daughter has grown up and written a children's story about her fear of the night, fuelled by her amazing imagination, and the great comfort of having her mother come in the door, as all of the creatures inhabiting her room would disappear.

Since we are told by Bahá'u'lláh that our children's concept of God is largely formed through their relationship with their parents, I don't think it is wise to give the child an impression that they are on their own when they have their little troubles. Bahá'u'lláh was said to have been concerned about His grandchildren's troubles, no matter how small. I love that example! Patience and the understanding that the child will soon outgrow these little habits can help parents find a balance between being totally at a child's mercy and showing kindness.

Irene Dominguez We paid attention to their cries from the very beginning. We never let them cry for long. We placed their crib next to our bed. I would attend to them right away.

Beth Bishop The eldest cried a lot until he was three months old. I tried to comfort him or kept him downstairs but on one occasion had to leave him to cry it out. We usually went and comforted them and then left the room but this was very difficult with the youngest who always wanted company. I used to bring the oldest into our bed but it then became difficult to get any sleep. So with the youngest, I used to go into her bed till she had gone to sleep and then go back to mine. For some years it was like musical beds.

Farzaneh Knight Contrary to many authorities, we never let them cry for long. They were immediately brought into our bed. We comforted and then returned them once they'd calmed down. I don't believe that children cry for no reason. Even if it can be called manipulative, the child needs the parents' love for whatever reason. It's the parents' job to give that to them. We feel the proof of the pudding is in the eating. Both daughters are extremely secure and independent as young adults. They are very close and loving to their parents.

Did you give your children an allowance?

Andrew Adams I give them money on a case-by-case basis. They do not receive an allowance.

Julie Young Our children were not given an allowance. Every week, they were given lunch money which was to last them the entire week. It was up to them to decide how to use that money. Sometimes they would make sandwiches and save their money. They received $20 a week lunch money when they were in high school.

Donna Smith Yes, they were given an allowance. We talked with them about dividing it into three parts – for the Faith, for savings and for themselves. We never told them how to divide it but just that they should divide it. They weren't responsible for paying for anything themselves until they were teens. At that point, they brought in money from their jobs. They were then responsible for their own money. They were given an allowance from a fairly young age.

Donald Pope Children need access to money if they are going to learn to manage it responsibly. I prefer that children have an opportunity to earn it by having extra job opportunities. I do not like the idea of children (particularly pre-adolescent children) getting an allowance without earning it. If they require or desire something, give them a way to earn it.

Katayun Golshani I did not give them an allowance. We had a rule in our household to make a distinction between needs and wants. If they needed something, they could come and present it to us. If we decided that that was a need, it would be provided no matter what. If it was a want, then we negotiated, looked at it and then decided if it was worth attending to or not. Some may say that this method won't teach children to budget. Staying within your budget is very important but really being able to identify your needs is an important principle. I'm not really sure if all we should be looking at as Bahá'ís is budgeting only according to the norms of a certain culture. Distinguishing one's needs and wants is the principle that we observe in order to pay Ḥuqúqu'lláh. We need to become familiar with that very early on. Our attitude should be, 'This is my need; why is it my need? How can I reduce my needs as much as possible?'

Angela Brown Every child should have some kind of allowance so he or she can feel a part of the household economy and learn to manage what funds they have. I always require each child, upon receiving a weekly allowance, to give to the fund, save a little for the bank, share a little with someone else and keep a little to spend as he wishes. This may sound like a lot but it really is a simple formula to learn how to link money with spirituality, generosity and economy. Sometimes, if a child hasn't done what he has been told, I might exact a small fine of 10 or 20 cents to let him know that this is not acceptable but with the understanding he is still learning.

Linda Bandari From the age of six our children received a small allowance. They had a piggy bank and saved for special things that they wanted. They gave a portion of that money to the Bahá'í fund. As they got a little older, they opened a savings account and put the money they got as gifts into the account. They managed to save up a significant amount of money by the time they went to college.

George and Mary Burke We give our children an allowance. Each child gets a different amount equal to what he or she would have to pay for basic necessities, such as snacks and supplies. Our seven year old gets four dollars per week, our ten year old gets five, and our 16 and 18 year olds get 20 each.

Lucy Matthews They say that allowances should not be connected with chores. I had an allowance, as did my daughter. As I grew older, it had to cover more things. We did the same thing with our daughter. At the beginning of each school year, we would change the allowance accordingly. We would sit down and tell her what it would have to cover.

Did you pay your children for chores?

Angela Brown As for chores and services, even the youngest child needs to learn how to serve in the simplest way – setting the table, taking out the trash, cleaning a room, dusting the furniture and feeding a pet. Children also need to know they are appreciated for their efforts to perform these services well or, if necessary, to redo them, if the results are not their best effort. Excellence in all things is the standard but little by little, step by step, they must learn and we must be patient and loving as we explain over and

CREATING A CONDUCIVE HOME ENVIRONMENT

over the same thing, until finally they have learned it. Getting paid for chores seems to take away the spirit of service.

Celia Stewart We didn't pay our children for chores. We felt that they should be of service to the family.

Kevin Johnson They were given an allowance that was based on their doing household chores from the time they were five. They were responsible for taking out the garbage, tidying the house and helping with the dishes.

Donald Pope Basic chores should be unpaid. Do the parents get paid for what they do around the house? If not, why should the children? If more money is required, a set of extra jobs that can be done for an agreed upon fee should do the trick.

John and Barbara Hartley In some instances, yes. In others, we told them they were expected to do things around the house because we were a family and everyone had an obligation to help out.

Linda Bandari Our children got a minimal amount of money for helping with chores around the house so that they could learn how to manage money. They were expected to help with chores as a part of living in our family, with or without an allowance. We all did chores to make our house a better place to live. We also did a lot of projects together. For example, my husband and son built a computer together when our son was nine.

Julie Young Our children did not have to do many chores. They were just too busy. Their only chore was to clean their rooms. When Feasts and other events were held at our home, we would collectively clean the house.

Joe and Wilma Thompson Only if it was above and beyond normal. They often wanted to make additional money and we would find yard work, garage cleaning or something to help them do so.

Margerie Gibson No! Chores are what we each contribute to the family's well-being. If she needs extra money for something, she has the option of doing small jobs for the neighbours. I cleared this with the neighbours first! She and I made up a flyer last year for her to take to all the houses near us with folks we know pretty well. She works in 15-minute increments, earning 25 cents for every 15 minutes. She pulls weeds, sweeps porches and helps with any small job around the house. Last summer she managed to earn an extra $15 to pay for goodies at the county fair!

What are you looking for in your child's choice of university? Do you have any concerns about college life?

> The academic life also has its fashions and fads, even though they are of a different nature from the fads of the man on the street.
> These fashions are not permanent; they are bound to change. Today the fad is a materialistic view of life and of the world. A day will soon come when it will become deeply religious and spiritual. In fact, we can discern the beginning of such a change in the writings of some of the most eminent souls and liberal minds. When the pendulum will start its full swing then we shall see all such eminent men turn again to God.[4]

Andrew Adams College is labelled as a training ground for young minds yet in reality it is a hotbed of hedonism. Our colleges are so morally bankrupt. Dormitories are riddled with alcohol, drugs and sex. Professors denigrate religious principles. They breed cynicism. Colleges seek to convert our young souls to the evils of secular materialism in the name of 'freedom'. Students are in danger of being exploited by the very university staff whose overt duty is to train and guide them. Nevertheless, our young Bahá'ís must be educated. They must develop a trade or profession. An

CREATING A CONDUCIVE HOME ENVIRONMENT

active Bahá'í community is an essential refuge for the young Bahá'í, who in many cases has left his home for the first time. Constant communication with parents and loved ones is indispensable.

Michelle Sharpe I have considered Nur University in Bolivia and, before it closed, considered Landegg Academy in Switzerland. We are determined to keep the Bahá'í standard. I am also interested in them learning other languages.

My first concern is sending them to large universities – I don't like the idea. My preference is that they be in a Bahá'í community. I feel that having Bahá'í peers is important. I feel the moral standards are extremely low in the non-Bahá'í world. I am amazed that some universities have such major problems as date rape, drinking, drugs, sex and so on. Moral leadership is absent. It would not be my first choice to send them to large colleges and universities in the US. Both our children are Canadians and may choose to attend Canadian universities. We are already familiar with two universities. Both have large Bahá'í communities and we know some students that have gone there. I would encourage mine to attend those.

My concern is that my children would be deprived of the continuation of a spiritual experience. There is so much emphasis on the physical world.

Donna Smith I believe that the child and parents should choose the university. The child should probably first choose and then consult about it with the parents. He is capable of maturity. He has to learn how to have the moral standard from within. For some children who are leaders, this is easy. For others who are followers, it is harder. For each situation, ongoing consultation with the parents will provide the safest route. I have concerns about society, about life overall. Society has turned very black and white. There are very high ideals and very low standards of behaviour. College is no different. By this age young adults should have the common sense and smarts to deal with it. They simply have to. We can't protect them. They have to be protected by their love of the Faith, the Covenant and love and respect for their parents. They will be okay if they have these in place. All this work is done long before they are teens.

Phoebe Untekar I think young people should choose their own universities, based on what type of degree programme they're looking for. By the time they are attending college, I should be able to trust their own judgement about the situations they will face.

Beth Bishop I would let them choose for themselves according to what subject they want to study. I would try to put them in touch with the local Baháʼís there. My eldest son never really participated in the Baháʼí community after he went to university. I think the life there is very difficult for them. They need the support of Baháʼí friends. My second son had friends he knew nearby. My daughter was already married when she started her course, which is in her home town.

Tom and Andrea Edwards I would definitely want our kids to be at a college with other Baháʼís if possible. We would steer away from co-ed dorms. Our concern is that college life is fraught with mental tests!

Linda Bandari In helping choose a university, I looked for one that was rated high in what my child wanted to major in; one that was fairly close to home so an occasional visit home was not too difficult or costly; one with affordable tuition; and one with a good reputation. There are Baháʼí communities near most universities, so a Baháʼí club was not a top priority of mine, although an added benefit. My children were involved in the selection process. We gathered information on the various universities of interest to them and then narrowed it down to three out-of-town visits. My main concern about college life was their safety. The first year I had my kids stay in a dormitory and after that they stayed in an apartment with a roommate. My daughter and I attended a self-defence course. I kept in contact with my children almost on a daily basis when they were at college and we still do today, even though they are married. The values instilled in my children through the years have carried through to adulthood. I feel fortunate that we never had any serious problems to deal with.

Simon Scott College life challenges any child's upbringing. It is simply going to happen as they are exposed to new and different ideas. If we have done our job, then we have established the limits of permissible behaviour and created a 'good conscience'. At that point, it is the college student's responsibility to make good decisions. They will make errors as all humans have. If they really believe in the standards by which they have been raised, they will survive and overcome. If they don't believe in the Bahá'í teachings and standards, then they will err. I wish them good luck.

In terms of choosing a college or university, it is based upon the child's educational needs and finances. The only exception to this might occur if I felt the attitude of an entire university was antipathetic to Bahá'í values. At that point, I would balk at giving approval to attend such an institution.

Katayun Golshani Having had three children in college and hearing from them, I know that unfortunately the college atmosphere has become a meat market rampant with sex, drugs and alcohol. These sit at the heart of college social life. It would be ideal for the child to spend the undergraduate years close to home. Although undergraduate children want to be independent, I think they need the love and support of their families, if possible. You should work with the child and consult with him in the decision-making process. You need to look for the types of courses and fields offered. It would also be good to visit the college to feel the atmosphere and the spirit of the college campus. Stay in touch with your children and be intimately close with them. Be available to them as they make friends. Help them. Be there for orientation. You should not allow a child to pick a certain college because of its 'fun life'. That's not a good road to follow. College clubs are very important and provide a wonderful support system. But it all depends on the child and the type of student.

BAHÁ'Í PARENTING PERSPECTIVES

Can you recommend your favourite parenting books?

Katayun Golshani I like Linda and Richard Eyre's books. They have a spiritual approach. Steven Covey also has a very spiritual approach. His *Seven Habits of Highly Effective Families* is a book, on tape and a CD. They're very much aligned with the teachings of the Faith. Scott Peck has some very good things that are also very helpful and complementary with the Bahá'í teachings. Any author that has a spiritual grounding is going to be far more on-track. If parents themselves do not know the writings, they're going to be very vulnerable and not prepared or equipped to pick the right material. They first need to know the writings themselves before they can be good judges. It's very good for parents to take parenting courses – such as the Bahá'í Core Curriculum parenting course. They then become educated consumers of parenting material. People spend so much time researching cars and homes before making a purchase. You have to know what's good and what's not. You need to distinguish and not just pick any book.

Melissa Taheri I've read most of the Bahá'í parenting books but don't have a favourite. One thing that helped was the question 'What would 'Abdu'l-Bahá do?'

Edyth Lewis There are a number of Bahá'í books about parenting: *Mothers, Fathers, and Children* by Furutan, *Education in the Bahá'í Family* by Hellaby, *Bahá'í Families* by Wilcox and *Family Repairs and Maintenance Manual* by Ghaznavi. These are all now out of print since they were very much set in the time that they were written. The challenges of parenthood have moved on, although each is worth reading still.

I found no non-Bahá'í book on parenting of any value at all but what I did find of tremendous value were two courses run by the Open University. One was called 'The Pre-school Child' and the other 'Childhood 5–10'. For each you were given what you should expect for normal development of a child across this age range but you were also encouraged to think about your own

CREATING A CONDUCIVE HOME ENVIRONMENT

values and what steps you need to take to instil certain values in your child. There were all sorts of games to play together as well. I suspect that the course no longer runs but there may be something similar.

Grace Simpson *Reviving Ophelia* by Mary Pipher.

Todd and Debbie McEwen Look at several books and choose the ones that suit you best. Don't rely on them to provide all the answers. The Bahá'í writings and your own instinct are the best source of parenting knowledge you can get. Between the two, they will generally give you far better answers than anything else.

Farzaneh Knight *The Family Virtues Guide*.

Michelle Sharpe *How to Talk So Kids Will Listen and Listen So Kids Will Talk* by Adele Faber and Elaine Mazlish. *The Violence-Free Family* by Hossain Danesh.

Andrew Adams My favourite parenting books are *The Advent of Divine Justice*, the *Bahá'í Education* compilation, *Bahá'í Marriage and Family Life* and Mr Furutan's book, *Mothers, Fathers, and Children*. Of course, the finest parenting books are the books that make us better persons and more spiritual. The more we can become transformed into spiritual individuals and develop our godlike sensibilities, the better parents we will be. Is there any other word that can transform us as can the creative Word of Bahá'u'lláh? We have to be the way we want our children to be.

Donald Pope No one should parent without the compilation *Bahá'í Education*. *The Family Virtues Guide* (could I not recommend it?). *The Magical Child* by Joseph Chilton Pearce. And the many books by the Christian psychologist Dr James C. Dobson.

Margerie Gibson Oh, yes! Some of my very favourites, in order of category are:

- Spiritual orientation: *Baháʼí Marriage and Family Life*; *Baháʼí Education*.
- Understanding the physical components of development: *Your Child's Growing Mind* by Jane Healy.
- Theory underlying relationships: *Children: The Challenge* by Rudolf Dreikurs, MD.
- Dreikur's theories in everyday language: *Positive Discipline for Preschoolers* and *Positive Discipline*, both by Jane Nelson.
- The title says it all!: *How to REALLY Love your Child* by Dr Ross Campbell. *How to Talk So Your Kids Will Listen and Listen So Your Kids Will Talk* by Adele Faber and Elaine Mazlish.
- Looking at family structure 'outside of the box': *The Family Bed* by Tine Thevenin.

Donna Smith Baháʼí books are a must. All books help somewhat but what really helps is using prayer, common sense, unity and consultation.

Bernice McKenzie I know I read a ton of them but I can't remember them. Isn't that funny? They were so important to me 30 years ago!

Richard and Theresa Baker Mr Furutan's book was quite helpful but sometimes I found it too idealistic. I think most of our good parenting (if that is what it can be called) was due to our Baháʼí values and good common sense and a good parental upbringing ourselves.

What sort of sacrifices did you have to make in order to parent the way that you saw fit?

Margerie Gibson I put off building a career until later in life. We used money for enrichment programmes for her, rather than spending it on things like movies, hobbies and newer cars. We

CREATING A CONDUCIVE HOME ENVIRONMENT

have chosen to stay in one location so that she can build lasting friendships with other children. We have given her the best and sunniest room in our house!

Edyth Lewis When the children were young I sacrificed a career in order to look after them. I have no regrets over this. Later, I always made sure that one of us, usually me, was available whenever they were home from school. My husband was an Auxiliary Board Member and frequently away from home at weekends, so it was up to me to create a stable atmosphere.

Linda Bandari The sacrifices that I made to parent the way I saw fit pales in comparison to the rewards that I am getting from having two great children. I have always placed my children and family as my number one priority, so career and personal things became secondary. As the kids grew older, I was still able to have my own business but always made a point of being home for dinner and taking them to their evening activities, helping them with homework and so on. We were a one-income household until our kids were school age. During those early years my husband quit his job and started his own business, so for a period of time we had very little income and it was a challenge to make ends meet. I felt that a good education was one of the most important things we could provide for our children, something that they could benefit from for their whole life. We enrolled our children in a very good private school starting when they were seven and eight years old. They attended that school until they graduated. Even though we had to simplify our life, it was worth it.

Beth Bishop Sometimes it was very difficult to enforce discipline, as my husband would not go along with me, so I had to compromise. On the other hand, he was often more relaxed when I might have been too strict on a point.

Nina Sadaghiyan I don't feel that I have sacrificed anything by being a parent. We decided to have children. Once that decision is made, it is natural to care for them and to do one's best to serve them. The child did not make a choice to be here.

Todd and Debbie McEwen We have made financial sacrifices. We have had less personal time and less freedom to do what we want when we want to do it. I have sacrificed my career. These are things that go with the responsibility of parenthood which you must accept as part of the 'job description'. It is better to look on it as an investment in your children's future and that of the following generation of grandchildren (if there are any).

Melissa Taheri I can't really think of sacrifices because I didn't feel I was sacrificing much. Time alone and time as a couple would probably be the major sacrifice.

Richard and Theresa Baker Sacrifices of time, mother not going out to work full time, less money, less sleep . . . A lot of effort on the part of both parents working together.

We sacrificed ourselves so that we could make sure that they went to Bahá'í youth activities when they were teenagers.

Simon Scott It hasn't seemed like much of a sacrifice thus far.

What, to you, is the most challenging issue(s) facing Bahá'í parents today?

> These Bahá'í children are of such great importance to the future. They will live in times, and have to meet problems, which never faced their elders. And the Cause alone can equip them to properly serve the needs of a future, war-weary, disillusioned, unhappy humanity. So their task will be very great and a very responsible one, and too much care cannot be devoted to their upbringing and preparation.[5]

Andrew Adams Without a doubt, the greatest challenge in raising

CREATING A CONDUCIVE HOME ENVIRONMENT

Bahá'í children today is the climate of materialism that children grow up in. Materialism breeds all of the qualities that we are trying to prevent our children from acquiring, specifically greed, selfishness, dishonesty and prejudice.

Katayun Golshani Establishing the Bahá'í identity of their children. If the children have their Bahá'í identity in place, the parents' job is really so much easier. If the parents don't establish this identity in their children, their children will be defective and will struggle for the rest of their lives in different ways. They'll be unable to comply with the will of their Lord. Ultimately, that's the whole goal, to know and to love God. Otherwise, children will get lost and destroyed by different influences. A parent's top priority should be to put their child's Bahá'í identity in place. This really has to do with the emotional context that the child experiences while living a Bahá'í life. I cannot stress this more. It is the emotional experiences that count. How do they feel when they are engaged in Bahá'í activities – whether it be worship, devotions, prayer or meetings? How do they feel rather than what is the content of the material? You don't spank a child and make them say a prayer. That prayer at that moment is no longer going to be serving the strengthening of the love of that child with Bahá'u'lláh. That kind of atmosphere will repel the child. You will be distancing the child from his Lord, rather than bringing him close. It is the emotional ties we create that count.

John and Barbara Hartley Raising a child with moral values and keeping him from indulging in drugs.

Farzaneh Knight Society. Keeping children protected from that hurricane of an environment that is obsessed with sex, looks, materialism, cliques, frivolity and cynicism – that are all raging out there. We were greatly aided by our circumstances, thanks to having gone pioneering; a small, watchful school; a somewhat more conservative society than in the US; and terrific schoolmates. If the household values are strong and practised by every member and if there is no hypocrisy or opposing rules and standards – such as one for private and one for public – children will not be confused. All these factors will shelter children from that hurricane outside.

Bernice McKenzie Building Bahá'í communities that their children want to be a part of, while at the same time being able to spend time with their children instead of always being at Bahá'í things.

Tom and Andrea Edwards Mental tests, moral laxity and liberal ideas.

Edyth Lewis I think parenting now is much more difficult than it was even 25 years ago. There is much more advertising 'in your face'. There is more sex and violence shown on television and moral standards have declined in that time.

Many young adults come from single parent families or families where the parents barely speak to each other. If a new parent comes from such a family then he or she has no model on which to base his own relationship.

Michelle Sharpe I feel the challenge is more internal than external. Developing a Bahá'í identity in the home is challenging; however, it is the foundation. I have observed some of the families in our community who have lost their youth. Many of these youth have no connection to the community. This is very revealing. The families that have youth with a vibrant Bahá'í identity are families that are teaching the Faith from the heart. Some of us have this Faith in our heads but it must be in our hearts. The most challenging part for parents is to be unified in the home. My children have told me many times that they love 19 Day Feasts that are presented in an interactive way. We have deepenings in our home every two weeks. The youth love to attend this, especially when we have a fun approach to teaching. Communication is so important. It is also essential to teach the love of Bahá'u'lláh.

On the external side, peer pressure is a concern. However, if

CREATING A CONDUCIVE HOME ENVIRONMENT

we are committed to the Faith our children and youth will reflect this. Developing spirituality in our children is quite a task in this material world.

Donald Pope Materialism and meaninglessness here in North America, its pervasiveness and how easily it is caught by our children.

Kevin Johnson Too much TV exposure; both parents working outside the home – hence far less interaction with children; and increasing depravity in movies and on television.

What are some of your tips for raising a spiritual and good child, a child with character?

Julie Young
1) Teaching and modelling prayer. Teaching them to have complete reliance in God.
2) Getting them to understand who Bahá'u'lláh is and to get a connection with Bahá'u'lláh. Bahá'u'lláh has to be in their hearts. They have to find Him very early on. You can't let them 'hit and miss' and you can't put this off until they're older.
3) Getting them to understand who 'Abdu'l-Bahá is. Share with them the Master, His stories and His life. Let them fall in love with Him and know that He is the perfect example. Teach them to look to the Master and never to you. As parents, we have to be detached. Always ask them, 'What would 'Abdu'l-Bahá do?'

Beth Bishop
1) Share the teachings with them and the pleasure of living a good life.
2) Appreciate their good qualities and encourage them in what they want to do.

3) Help them grow up as part of the Bahá'í community that gives them a great feeling of security and many friends.
4) Make them aware that they have a duty to serve the Cause and their fellow beings and not just do what they want to.
5) Help them to think globally.

Simon Scott It is clear to me that they need, if not daily, then very frequent explanations of why the values that Bahá'u'lláh reiterates or enunciates are superior to the values common today. One cannot depend on 'do this' or 'don't do that' as good enough explanations. The rationale must be understood and explained by the parent to the child's/teenager's satisfaction. Then it gets tough, as the parent must live up to these standards as an example. Make no mistake. Kids will note and reject the values of a parent whose actions are not in agreement with the values that they try to instil. Remember, 'actions speak louder than words'.

Nina Sadaghiyan
1) Set a good example for your children.
2) Don't say one thing and do another.
3) Stick to the Bahá'í writings and keep them close at all times.
4) Be patient.
5) Spend time with your children.

Todd and Debbie McEwen
1) Give your children time and attention.
2) Treat them with respect as individuals, while still maintaining your parental role.
3) Give them a good grounding in the Bahá'í writings, treating the writings as the standard for all behaviour.
4) Give them a firm framework of expected behaviour from the earliest age, being consistent about your expectations of obedience.
5) Do not give them a lot of rules to follow, but those that you do have must be obeyed.

CREATING A CONDUCIVE HOME ENVIRONMENT

6) Gradually give them more responsibility to monitor their own standards as they grow older and become more mature.
7) Don't expect to find rigid rules about any situation. Use your common sense, together with the Bahá'í writings, your knowledge of your own child and a degree of flexibility.
8) Consult with your children. Ask for their input and explain to them why you make your decisions.
9) Example is always best. Behave in an appropriate way, so your children are able to behave well too. Use the Bahá'í writings as the baseline for your own behaviour as well as that of the children.

Bernice McKenzie
1) Love them with all your heart and soul.
2) Pray with them.
3) Encourage them.
4) Laugh with them.
5) Tell them every day how important they are to you.
6) Really, really like them.
7) Pray for them.
8) When you do something wrong, apologize to them.
9) Love them with all your heart and soul.

Phoebe Untekar I asked my kids what it was in their lives that allowed them to become who they are today. They all said pretty much the same thing: that we set the example of unquestioned faith in Bahá'u'lláh and that it was simply a part of their lives. We saw tests as a natural part of life and talked a lot about that dynamic.

Margerie Gibson
1) Read, *read, read*! Study every parenting book you can get your hands on. Start before you even get pregnant! Keep the things that resonate with you and scrap the rest.
2) Snuggle your kids – for more than five minutes every morning upon awaking, often throughout the day, and ten or so

minutes every night before sleeping. They never get too much loving.
3) Love your spouse a lot. Seeing their parents cuddling each other, with an open invitation for the kid to climb into the huddle, is the best, most reassuring thing in a kid's life.
4) Take time to be together as a family. Even Bahá'í activities don't count here. Go off by yourselves at least once per month to do something with just your family. Don't bring friends along, either adult or other kids. Just your family.
5) Include friends in just about everything else – dinner, movies, gardening, service projects and exercise.
6) Make a specific date each week for whichever parent is home the least (usually dad) with each child. My daughter and husband have 'Daddy/Daughter Date Day' every Saturday morning. They walk down to the local coffee shop and get a treat, read a chapter or two from whatever read-aloud they're working on, then walk home again. In warm weather they might go out to the playground at the park or on an outing in a country area. My sister's husband rotated the date with their three girls, a different one each week.
7) Work together as a family team. We garden together and clean the house together.
8) Pray together as a family. Attend Feast together, say obligatory prayers together and study the scriptures together.
9) Talk about everything. Think out loud, showing the processing of your own thoughts. Teach by your example of how you think through your decisions. Allow your child to hear you work through bad ideas and work towards good ones. Let them learn from watching your own spiritual struggles in action. Let them watch you make the right choices, while hearing how you consider all the choices. One small example. When at a store, you find a nice jacket left lying on a bench and it's just your size. You verbally say, 'Hmmm . . . I could use a nice jacket like this but whoever it belongs to would be unhappy to have lost it, huh? Let's find some way to get this jacket back to whoever it belongs to, okay?' Then go together and find a lost-and-found

CREATING A CONDUCIVE HOME ENVIRONMENT

or something. This way, they see you battle with temptation, win and choose to do the right thing. It's a great way to help them learn to work through those choices themselves.
10) Respect your children. They are God's creations, too, not just yours. Respect your spouse and speak respectfully to each other. Speak respectfully to your children, to model respectful speech for them. If you don't, you will hear your own 'tone' of voice come right back at you in short order. Respect yourself. Treat yourself well. Take care of your needs – physical, spiritual and mental. They learn their whole way of being from you. Model a good one.

Edyth Lewis
1) Do what feels natural to you – follow your heart.
2) Pray together and read the writings morning and evening.
3) Make sacrifices. This is the most important job in the world.
4) Read stories together. There are some good Bahá'í books for children and some good non-Bahá'í ones too.
5) Laugh with your children and find ways of having fun together.
6) Encourage your child to have Bahá'í friends as well as non-Bahá'í ones.
7) Don't bow to peer (your own) pressure.
8) Don't expect your children to be perfect and don't be embarrassed when they are not. Your goal is for them to be good adults.
9) Keep talking to your child even through times when you fear that the relationship may have broken down. This should be a true dialogue, not you telling him what he should or should not be doing.
10) Turn the TV off and talk to each other.

Donald Pope
1) If you are not willing to make the development of a child's character your first priority for the first five years in his life, think twice about having children now.

2) Be a constant presence in your child's life.
3) Live a life of purpose and involve your children in that life.
4) Mention God every day and live in the presence of the Almighty every moment of every day.
5) If your children are not strong enough to resist the materialism in the world in which they live, relocate to a setting where people matter more than things.
6) Let no virtue go unacknowledged, let no lapse go without a call for the missing virtue.
7) Set clear boundaries and reasonable consequences before they are needed.
8) Be consistent and trustworthy. You promise, you deliver, you threaten, you act.
9) Be a parent, a protector/authority in service of the child's learning and development.
10) Never forget that you are raising one of God's children. Show respect, listen and then act as if God is your judge (He is).

If you could parent all over again and knowing what you know now, what would you do differently? How would you advise 'brand new' parents today?

Julie Young I would read Bahá'í books every evening as a family all the way through from early childhood until they leave home. Read not only the sacred texts together but other Bahá'í books – biographies, history and so on. One family that I know has always done this with their now grown children. Even if they are tired, they still sit down together and read just a short passage every evening.

Margerie Gibson I would urge parents to *slow down*! Don't be in such a rush to make your kids grow up. Let them play freely, take them for hikes in the woods or to the beach, wherever nature is free near you. Get rid of television. Even educational TV sucks kids into the mindless realm of brain-dead-zombies-in-front-of-

CREATING A CONDUCIVE HOME ENVIRONMENT

the-tube. Start reading to them from the time they're about four months old. Brace yourself for massive multiple readings of every favourite book your child finds and be grateful that she wants you to read to her. Don't be in a rush to place them in special 'classes' for early readers or anything early. Just *be* with them. They love it.

Grace Simpson I would do the same thing all over again. What worked for me was our time together every morning before she went to school. We would say prayers and read the writings. This was expected and we did it.

Simon Scott Personal transformation spiritually so that they are an example that their children want to emulate.

John and Barbara Hartley I would be more patient and spend more time with them. Children grow up very quickly and parents should savour every moment. Loving them unconditionally and telling them they are loved works. Getting into a 'power struggle' does not work. Giving them choices does.

Richard and Theresa Baker I don't think we would have changed much. We absolutely loved both our children from the start and we gave ourselves to them as parents. We always had time for them and we tried to impart to them spiritual values.

What worked best was love and encouragement and constant prayer for their well-being and achievements.

One thing we didn't do, and I think should have done, was to have set aside a time each day for some kind of a family devotional.

We would advise always having an open house for our children to invite their friends to.

Michelle Sharpe What I would do differently is to never have an argument in front of them. For the sake of unity I would end the argument and come back to the situation with solutions. I would recognize and manage my anger, avoid being judgemental and show more empathy. Learning how to consult has helped us greatly.

Nina Sadaghiyan I would do the same but I would try to be more patient. I would advise brand new parents to avoid spoiling their children. If you work outside the home, you should avoid buying them gifts and trying to buy their love out of feelings of guilt. You will run out of ideas and money. The key is to spend as much time with them as you can. That is what they remember. Make sure they know they are the most *important* in your life. Be there for them.

Andrew Adams I cannot say that I would do anything differently, were I to begin raising my kids again. I have done my best to raise them according to Bahá'í principles. The rest is up to them. To parents beginning to raise their kids today, I would advise using a good mix of spiritual principles and common sense. It is vital that the parents support one another. They must be entirely united, commit themselves to each other. Work out differences in parenting ideas in private. The child must be shown that the relationship between his mother and father is rock solid. This provides reassurance to the child. Many disagreeable situations can be entirely avoided. One other extremely important rule is that parents have happy, loving relationships with their own parents – the child's grandparents. This models a productive parent–child relationship. Parents must never criticize their own parents or the parents of their spouse.

Donna Smith I wouldn't do much differently.
My advice for parents today is to take care of your marriage. Put your marriage first. Children want a strong union. They do not need indulgent parents. Also, remember to parent. Do not let the child be the parent.
The things that worked were discipline, prayer, consultation, fun, family outings, as many Bahá'í events as possible and love.
The things that did not work were anger, giving up, indulging and ignoring signs of problems.

CREATING A CONDUCIVE HOME ENVIRONMENT

Parenting is the hardest job you will ever do. It is the greatest responsibility you will ever shoulder. The price is a human soul. You are all things. You are a teacher, lover, parent and servant 365 days a year for many years. You will be tired when it is finished but you will know you did your job as best as you could. And God doesn't ask any more from you.

8

Meet the Children

How do you think the Bahá'í Faith has affected you throughout your life?

Negin Golshani When I was a child I think the Bahá'í Faith sheltered me and provided me with a solid foundation and identity, enabling me to make healthy decisions later in life.

When I was a teenager the Faith was like a railing of string along a very steep and narrow path; the guidance was there but it would only work if I acknowledged it and consciously chose to follow it.

In retrospect, I can see that there were times when, if not for the influence of the Bahá'í Faith and other strong Bahá'í youth, I would have changed for the worse, or missed an opportunity to change for the better, and I'm infinitely glad I'm a Bahá'í.

Helen Thompson When I was a child I basked in the glow of my love for Bahá'u'lláh, thanks to daily exposure to prayer and the Bahá'í lifestyle.

When I was a teenager, while my obedience to the Faith was constantly being tested (peer pressure, etc.), my parents provided the best kind of boat that I needed to weather out this storm of confusion and emotional conflict. On this boat were different virtues: openness, honesty and understanding. I never felt that I couldn't talk to them about something, which helped immensely.

I feel that I matured, in every sense, earlier than most people because of the Faith and my parents. I never desired or seized the opportunity to put myself in danger (finances, exploring relationships with the opposite sex, using judgement in making friends) because I knew better from the writings and the parental advice I received on a regular basis through phone or email.

Andrew Lewis When I was a child the Faith gave me better values. But I guess that it's difficult to say.
When I was a teenager the Faith made my life more of a challenge. I had all these conflicting thoughts, feelings and urges and I couldn't be like my friends.
I am now a stronger person, with something to give to society. I feel I am much more positive and solution-oriented than many people in British society. This is all thanks to the Bahá'í Faith.

Katie Burke When I was a child I felt like I had two separate lives: one at school and with the outside world and another with the world that the Bahá'í teachings painted in my mind.
As a teenager I've started to put the two worlds together and balance my life. I realize that my Bahá'í goals help shape my earthly goals. The Faith has set me apart from my peers and given me my identity. I now find people who are searching for truth and I appreciate being able to share the teachings of the Faith with these thirsting souls.

David McEwen As a child I had a very definite standard of morals and I also knew that I was different from other people because I was a Bahá'í.
Now that I am a teenager, the Bahá'í Faith gives me a purpose, a sense of place and perspective, both in life and among my friends. It is very much a part of who I am, and my friends accept this and recognize that it is important to me.

Shirin Sadaghiyan The only things I remember about the Bahá'í Faith from my childhood is going to Sunday school and memorizing Bahá'í prayers.
I know that my parents instilled blessed virtues within my

brother and me that came from the principles of the Bahá'í Faith. However, I don't think that the Bahá'í Faith itself actually grabbed me until my late teenage years. I declared when I was 17 years old. For the first time in my life I realized that the Bahá'í Faith was the life I needed. I actually felt awakened and I was so on fire. I can't explain exactly why it happened at this particular time in my life but I think it had a lot to do with the sudden explosion of Bahá'í energy around me.

Since I've been an adult the Bahá'í Faith has led to me focus more on long-term aspects such as getting married and having a family. I have also been concentrating on what career path I would like to take.

How is your life different from the life of your non-Bahá'í friends?

Deborah Oliver My life has a definite direction and focus. I have no plans for myself and every decision I make about my life I make only through intense prayer and after consultation with Dad and Jackie. Often, others have goals for their personal fame but little or no direction. The Bahá'í teachings are the framework for how I should live.

Laili Pfingston There is a focus and centredness in my life, more optimism about humanity and a greater appreciation for diversity. The most permanent and spiritually rewarding results have come from the Bahá'í teachings.

Zhinous Knight I feel like there is a purpose for my life. My non-Bahá'í friends seem so empty inside. They are searching for something but they don't know what. The Bahá'í teachings have affected all of my decisions and they serve as a guide for making the right decisions.

Negar Knight *So* many things! To be totally honest, I think my life is a lot easier because I feel that I have more of a sense of purpose which really keeps me from doing things that many non-Baháʼís might indulge in – such as drinking alcohol, sex, drugs and so on. And I see that a lot of my friends don't really have a sense of meaning in their lives. They don't even understand why they're alive, whereas I'm just constantly trying to find out how to fulfil my sense of purpose. The teachings of the Baháʼí Faith have been the source of my morality and my sense of who I am. I don't even want to imagine what my life would be like without the Baháʼí Faith.

Jennifer Thompson Well, it is different in all ages. When I was younger, I didn't see anything different but as I got older I could see the difference in our morals and daily beliefs. I wholly believe that the Baháʼí teachings *protected* me!

Helen Thompson I feel that my experiences throughout my life, especially as an adolescent and young adult, differed in that I was protected from making mistakes that my other non-Baháʼí friends made by having the Faith as a form of guidance and direction.

Academically, I was especially interested in the sciences (I graduated from college with a BA in Biology and Sociology) because they were highly extolled by our Faith and because both my father (a physician) and mother (a dental hygienist) had careers in the medical field and derived a lot of satisfaction from them.

Socially, the Baháʼí teachings affected my decisions because I knew that it was important how I led my life, as an example to others, for it is the most effective way of teaching.

Spiritually, my decisions as a young woman led me to my husband (we met at a Baháʼí conference in Orlando) and inevitably led me and my husband to create our family, our daughter Beth, together. It also led me to remain active in our Baháʼí community through serving on our newly created local spiritual assembly here, as well as becoming part of our Ruhi study circle.

Katie Burke Everything I do from day to day has a purpose and a meaning, whereas many of my non-Baháʼí friends do things for no reason. As I get older, I appreciate my Bahá'í background more and more because I have answers to my questions and my life has a great purpose. It's comforting to feel this, especially during my teenage years when many things are uncertain or unclear. The Bahá'í teachings have always had an effect on my decisions, especially in the last couple of years, ever since I reached the age of maturity.

Leila Peters My life seems happier and more fulfilling than that of the non-Bahá'ís around me.

Andrew Lewis I have a very different perspective on the purpose of life. And I have had many opportunities to do things that I might not have had. Also, mixing with people who have a 'healthy' outlook on life certainly helps you to feel more positive. In practical terms this means less wasting time in pubs and bars, more travel, more contact with people from all over the world, a much greater 'global' perspective and less racism and xenophobia.

Shamim Sadaghiyan I care about a lot of things that they don't care about. There are a lot of materialistic distractions that occupy a lot of their time and their concept of chastity is very low. I don't think it matters, though. A lot of my Bahá'í friends are the same. The Bahá'í teachings did guide my decisions. They have ultimately had a direct impact on my attitude to life. I have been blessed to have grown up in a Bahá'í family.

David McEwen My life is different in some respects and the Bahá'í teachings do provide guidance. For instance, I strive to avoid backbiting and to steer people away from doing it. I also try to maintain a high moral standard. But one of the reasons that the people in my friendship group are my friends is because they too have high moral standards and strong personalities and so my standards are often like those of the rest of the group.

Shirin Sadaghiyan It's hard to think how my life is different from

MEET THE CHILDREN

that of my friends because I don't tend to focus on that particular aspect. But it is obvious that there are differences between my life and those of my friends who are not Bahá'ís. My daily habits and behaviour differ from some of my non-Bahá'í friends in respect of what they do to have a good time, such as drinking, having sex and so on. However, I have noticed that my closest friends live the Bahá'í life even though they aren't Bahá'ís.

One of the main differences is that our religions are not the same. Nonetheless, they are all one and I notice that right away because we discuss the similarities of our respective faiths without debate, as we should.

I truly believe that the Bahá'í Faith has guided me to live the life I live today. I think that my life choices fit quite nicely into the necessary obligations of the Faith.

Ariane Dominguez Just the fact that we don't drink or do drugs, which are so common nowadays, makes us different. People know and respect that.

What are some of your favourite books and why are they your favourites?

Deborah Oliver It's hard to answer this because I've just recently begun to delve into the writings personally and those that I've read in the past year are the best books to me. I'm sure that when I read more, those books will be equally important to me. Recently I've read *Some Answered Questions*, some of the *Kitáb-i-Íqán*, *Lights of Guidance* and compilations on detachment, love and happiness. I can't put into words why they are so special to me, they just are. Read them (if you haven't) and you'll understand why.

Laili Pfingston *God Loves Laughter* by William Sears, *Táhirih* by Clara A. Edge and *To Kill a Mockingbird* by Harper Lee. All these books were motivating and had moral points.

BAHÁ'Í PARENTING PERSPECTIVES

Negar Knight Hmmm. I love courtroom dramas and suspense novels so anything by James Patterson or John Grisham usually really appeals to me. I also love the book *The Diary of Juliet Thompson*, which is about the life of one of the earliest American believers in the Bahá'í Faith. I think I like it so much because the book is so real and emotional and tender, especially when she talks about 'Abdu'l-Bahá.

Zhinous Knight *God Loves Laughter* by William Sears. This book is full of life. I love Mr Sears. I also like John Grisham novels because they are about law, which interests me a lot. His books are very captivating.

Negin Golshani *Pride and Prejudice* because the protagonist (Elizabeth) is feminine, yet strong and intelligent. Unlike the women around her, marriage is not her life goal.

Trevor Adams *To Kill a Mockingbird*. This book is a great depiction of so many controversial issues.

Jennifer Thompson For a devoted bookworm that is a tough question! I love non-fiction, autobiographical and history books. They give you wisdom and truth behind the history and you learn from people's experiences.

Helen Thompson *From Copper to Gold,* about Dorothy Baker, is a very inspirational story about one of our first female Bahá'ís. *Mists of Avalon* by Marion Zimmer Bradley is a fantasy novel which incorporates a lot of the Bahá'í teachings, such as the oneness of mankind and the oneness of God, in subtle ways.

Katie Burke *To Kill a Mockingbird* because it introduced me to injustice. *Slaughterhouse-Five* because it's absurd and presents the reality of war. *Pride and Prejudice* because it's girly and because I love period pieces.

MEET THE CHILDREN

Shamim Sadaghiyan *The Dawn-breakers* is my favourite book because it brings the early history of the Faith to life. It made me aware of the sacrifice that the early believers made to bring the Faith out of obscurity. *God Passes By* is also a wonderful book, for the same reason.

Linda Paulson I read romance novels mostly and I read them because they always have a happy ending and people fall in love. They are fairytales, I know, but I am a hopeless romantic and can't help it!

David McEwen I enjoy science fiction and fantasy and like *The Wheel of Time* series by Robert Jordan because of the rich world that was created in the books.

Shirin Sadaghiyan I have read so many that it's hard to remember all of them but there are a few that stand out in my mind.

One book I read in my elementary school years that I have not forgotten is Katherine Paterson's *Bridge to Terabithia*. It touched me so much. It was the first book I ever read that turned a moment of tragedy and loss into happiness and gain. It is truly a beautiful story that emphasizes the unity of people despite their differences.

Invisible Man by Ralph Ellison is my ultimate favourite novel of all time! I read it in high school, in my senior year. It's a book written about an African-American youth who searches for an identity for himself. It's absolutely beautiful and it has inspired me to learn more about myself.

The last book that really stands out in my mind is one I read just a few months ago. The book *Crick Crack, Monkey* by Trinidadian writer Merle Hodge is an extraordinary story about the struggle women go through in a colonialist educational system. I really enjoyed this particular work because it taught me how the imposition of one culture upon another can result in greater and unnecessary prejudice among people of one family, showing that prejudice only breaks families apart rather than making them stronger.

Ariane Dominguez I read *The Alchemist* a little while ago. The story was simply fascinating and made me think about spirituality.

Mullá Husayn because it taught me so much about Bahá'í history and made me realize how little we are doing and how much can be done.

Thief in the Night shows the greatness of the Cause and how the Bible prophesies the coming of the Báb and Bahá'u'lláh so clearly.

Heidi is a very nice book. It shows the kindness in the heart of a little girl.

Were your career plans affected by the Bahá'í teachings?

Laili Pfingston Yes. I needed to find something that would benefit mankind and be of service to humanity, something that would be in accordance with the teachings. Otherwise, there was no point in me having that career.

Zhinous Knight No. I always wanted to do something that I could use to help the Faith but my decision was not affected by the Bahá'í teachings.

Negin Golshani As yet, I have no career but the Bahá'í teachings play a strong role in my decision. I have been taught to highly value service to humanity, thus I want a job that gives me the feeling that I am doing something to help others. Also, I want a job that is flexible enough to allow me to have a family. I don't need to relinquish the privilege of motherhood in order to prove my equality to men because I have learned that we can be equal in our differences.

Helen Thompson Yes. As I pointed out, becoming a teacher and studying the arts and sciences is greatly extolled. I was a high school science teacher for two years and loved every bit of it. If I had a nickel for every time I recognized the parallel between science and religion and taught that to the class, I'd be a millionaire by now. It gave me huge pleasure knowing that I was opening up not only worlds of science to these young adults but worlds of spirituality as well. Even though I had to teach such concepts in a subtle manner, witnessing their minds grasp them was invaluable beyond thought.

Shirin Sadaghiyan I don't have a career yet but I can say that what I have chosen to pursue has a lot to do with the teachings of the Bahá'í Faith. I have always had a passion for writing and I hope to get a Master's in journalism so that I can write about ways and means of uniting and advancing civilization rather than the negative side of humanity. After that, I hope to become a university professor teaching with the Bahá'í writings as my foundation for my approach and subject matter. So I am not exactly there yet but I know that God will guide me in the direction that He knows is best for me.

What will you do differently when you are a parent?

Helen Thompson Nothing! The only thing that may be different is how Beth will see the world, as opposed to how I saw it growing up. Being Joe and Wilma's daughter was a bit unique. I feel that my deafness helped protect me from a lot of our society's 'spoken garbage' and I have mentally prepared myself in that Beth, as a hearing child, will not be protected from such things. So, in that sense, I will have to do something different in that I will have to deal with Beth's view of the world which is different from mine. Other than that, I do not plan on doing anything different. I am totally in sync with how my parents see discipline and self-esteem, and in how you should treat others in the way you want to be treated.

Andrew Lewis My wife and I are really keen to instil a strong Bahá'í identity in our children. We decided to be less active in celebrating Christmas and to focus our attention and excitement on the Bahá'í festivals and Holy Days. We also want to help our children understand Bahá'í life and we want to use the Virtues Project and so on.

As for the reality of this, we shall see how well we do after all the sleepless nights!

Shirin Sadaghiyan I know that there are things that I say I would do differently but they will most likely change once I actually become a parent myself. Growing up with my parents, I have learned that the world is a scary place and no parent wants to see her child exposed to such things. Nonetheless, there will be a time when that child must face the world and all the tests and trials it has to offer. I think when I am a parent I will definitely be protective of my children but, in the same instance, I don't want to shelter them from the outside world. There will be times when they will face things that will be beyond my control and I will have to understand and accept that.

What do you appreciate most about your parents?

Deborah Oliver Their openness in sharing their love and their giving. I love that they're the best examples for me to strive to follow.

Laili Pfingston Their unconditional love and support, the way that they have taught by their example and their trust in me.

Negar Knight That they always put my needs and my sister's before theirs. And that they are so active in the Faith because they have set the standard for me.

Zhinous Knight The fact that they have always been there for me and that they have planted the seed of love for the Faith in my heart.

Negin Golshani My parents are reasonable. They don't make me do things 'just because'. They don't put up a wall of false politeness that makes them untouchable and me a victim of their mandates but instead they give me quite a lot of freedom. They are only strict about things that really matter. Also, they aren't close-minded and are willing to change. On the other hand, they are also responsible and maintain firm values. I am so amazed when I hear about other families and their intolerance of interracial marriage or lack of support for their children going abroad and so on. My parents pretty much fully support everything that doesn't contradict the Bahá'í writings!

Trevor Adams Communication galore!

Jennifer Thompson Very loving, open, trustworthy and generous.

Helen Thompson Two things: They are Bahá'ís. And they are truly *mankind lovers*. While I wish I could say that both of these mean the same thing, my experiences with other Bahá'ís, unfortunately, have revealed to me that such a thing isn't realistic.

Andrew Lewis Their tolerance and support and the freedom they allowed us to discover ourselves.

Katie Burke Their support and care.

Shamim Sadaghiyan That they are the only people on the planet who will always be there for us. I appreciate their love and encouragement.

Linda Paulson My mother and stepfather are always willing to help out when I need them the most. My father loves to tell his stories about his mother's father as well as answer any questions I have.

David McEwen They are supportive of me and also supportive of my friends when they have troubles.

Shirin Sadaghiyan My parents have done so much for me that it's rather difficult to just remember one thing I appreciate the most. However, the one thing that I cannot deny is their loving and helpful support. No matter what I choose to do, they are always there to support me. I appreciate that so much. Their support motivates me and I feel that they trust my judgement and that makes me more confident about myself. It allows me to grow and develop even further so that I may learn how to pass the tests of life on my own two feet; and if I need the help, they are always there to be of some assistance.

Ariane Dominguez I like it when I can tell them something that I did wrong and they don't get angry. They have always told me to tell them whenever something's wrong and that they wouldn't get overly upset. They would rather hear it from me than from someone else. When I approach them, they don't get angry. They either give me advice or ask me why I did something and I tell them. It is very nice. Also, we are able to tell them when we don't like something that they're doing. We consult about these things.

What do you appreciate least about your parents?

Laili Pfingston The guilt trips and feelings of disappointment they have when I have done something less than satisfactorily.

Negar Knight They're very busy all the time!

Zhinous Knight They still view me as a child sometimes. I feel that I am no longer that child they see.

Negin Golshani They are a bit critical of others. I think in teaching me how lucky I am to be a Bahá'í, they also conditioned me to be a bit arrogant and it's difficult to undo, even if you are conscious of it.

MEET THE CHILDREN

Jennifer Thompson Tendency to jump to conclusions.

Andrew Lewis Sometime I wish they were a little more proactive. Sometimes it takes them a long time to get things done but I put that down partly to how much work they have to do. When I was a child, I wished they could have been a bit more affectionate sometimes.

Katie Burke Their busy schedules.

David McEwen They can have fixed views on certain subjects.

Shirin Sadaghiyan The thing I appreciate least about my parents is that they are too protective of me at times. Sometimes I feel when I encounter specific situations my parents don't perceive them in the same way I do. The Persian culture has a strong influence in their thinking, since they were raised in Iran. So the particular experiences they share with me may be completely different from mine because they are coming from a different cultural context. I would just like them to look at things from a broader perspective. I know it's hard to do that, though, when one is used to doing things in another way. At the same time, I should be understanding about where they are coming from as well. It goes both ways.

Ariane Dominguez They probably don't realize this but they sometimes tell us to do or to stop doing something when there's someone else in the house.

Looking back, what do you think are the most important things you've learned from your parents?

Deborah Oliver I learned from them that I am always loved. I learned a way of living and growing from my tests and being a happy and joyful being but not suppressing my emotions. I learned to feel and to bring things up to those who need to hear them in order to better a situation, or to record my feelings in a journal as a form of release. I've learned so many skills to live life the way I want to that it is impossible to name them all. I also learned that there's only so much that parents can give you. You must take your own initiative to become closer to God.

Laili Pfingston Putting Bahá'u'lláh and His teachings at the centre of my life, appreciating diversity, being loving, valuing education, creating and maintaining a strong family unit, being trustworthy and being responsible.

Negar Knight Everything! They've taught me so much. I guess the most important things would be my religion, morality, virtues and love.

Zhinous Knight I think the most important thing I have learned from them is that if you serve Bahá'u'lláh, He will take care of you.

Negin Golshani That's a hard one. I learned to constantly examine myself; never to be content with who I am at the moment but to strive always to improve; to seek information; and to be an active participant. They taught me to take initiative and to be considerate of others; and when I see shortcomings in others, instead of dwelling on those shortcomings, to try to fix those things in myself. I learned to 'pick my battles' and once I've picked them, to fight long and hard. I learned not to tolerate injustice and to stand up for what I believe in. I also learned how to communicate.

Trevor Adams My dad taught me to listen.

Jennifer Thompson Being honest.

Helen Thompson Consultation. Communication. Cooperation.

Katie Burke To do my best at whatever I'm doing. To look at the big picture in every situation and keep in mind how the activities of my youth will affect my future. Not to take anything too seriously. To remember that 'dating leads to mating', so be rational with my emotions – ha ha! My parents have especially taught me to see myself as a world citizen and to feel responsible for the future of our planet. Since I turned 13 they have organized my summers in advance to make sure I travel somewhere new and help people in other places. Travelling away from my parents at such a young age made me very aware of the world and forced me to decide what role I was going to play in it. It was hard at times but all good things are, I guess.

Shamim Sadaghiyan To love and respect everyone, no matter who they are or where they come from. To always be happy in life because otherwise you are wasting your time.

Linda Paulson To never argue in front of children because it affects and hurts them as much as it affects and hurts you. Always pray to Bahá'u'lláh and God for guidance and answers. But more than anything, I learned to love people for who they are now, not what they've done, not their past, but who they are right now. To always find something good about a person. It's always there, you just have to look hard enough. I also learned that it's okay to cry whether you're a man or a woman.

David McEwen I think that my parents have taught me to be an individual, and not to blindly follow the crowd.

Shirin Sadaghiyan My parents have taught me so much about life and the most important thing they have taught me is love. Love is such a beautiful force and I have realized that with love anything positive can and will be accomplished. Out of their love, my parents have sacrificed so much to make the lives of my brother and me much more comfortable and manageable. The Bahá'í Faith has always been a strong foundation in our household and if it were not for the Bahá'í writings, I probably would not have appreciated my parents as much as I do.

BAHÁ'Í PARENTING PERSPECTIVES

How do you feel about your future?

Deborah Oliver I feel that God is working miracles and I will end up where I am supposed to be. My immediate plans are to go to school at the University of Washington and major in Bahá'í Studies as an undergraduate and in children's education as a graduate degree. My only real hope for the next ten years is that my own ego will not inhibit God's will from being done.

Laili Pfingston I feel confident, excited and scared, considering that I am graduating from university in a few months. I don't know exactly what I will be doing right after – whether I will be working, doing a little travelling or serving in small Bahá'í projects near my city or state.

As for the next ten years, I plan on seeing more parts of the world, learning more languages, furthering my academic education, getting married and having children – but not necessarily in that order.

Negar Knight Hmmm, a little bit uncertain but excited and still a little sad for the things I might be leaving behind once I graduate. My immediate plans are to go to college and to get a higher education. My hopes for the next ten years are to graduate from college, to be married, to have a career and I want to definitely be thinking about children. I want to be able to serve the Faith as best as possible.

Negin Golshani I feel so very unsure about the future! But that's not a source of worry – trust in God is a beautiful thing! My immediate plans are to graduate from college and choose a fulfilling career. My plans for the next ten years are to get married and move out of the US. I am slowly learning that the kind of career I choose must be interpersonal and also give me a channel to serve humanity. If I don't feel I'm helping the world, then my job is a waste of time. As to exactly how I will do that, I am not sure.

MEET THE CHILDREN

Trevor Adams I look so forward to the future! I can't wait to do everything, starting with being a fire paramedic!

Jennifer Thompson Wonderful! Exciting! My immediate plans are that I hope to get into a Master's programme starting this year to become a science teacher. I am still waiting on word from the school about whether I have been accepted. My hope for the next ten years is to start a family.

Helen Thompson My future couldn't be any better at this point. I am content in my full-time mothering duties and part-time contract work with a deaf organization writing for their newsletter. My daughter is growing up in a happy and stable environment. She has two parents who love her very much, as well as extended family members who support and care for her. Jeff and I are part of an intimate Bahá'í community (12 members at present) as well as an extended metro Bahá'í community with over 200 members. We feel as if we have the best of both worlds. Tonight, as a matter of fact, we are hosting the very first Feast our community has ever had! History is in the making as we speak! Jeff and I are also looking forward to our next baby, which we will start trying for during next year. Our marriage is blessed, for we certainly are the best of friends and partners in every sense.

Andrew Lewis I feel generally positive about the future. I am enjoying being a father and I am looking forward to the birth of my second child very shortly. We're also working on setting up a Bahá'í based business. I hope that in ten years' time we will be successful and that we can be a strong Bahá'í family and in a position to help others.

Katie Burke I'm excited! I feel there are a lot of new and wonderful opportunities for me in these next years. Right now I am finishing my junior year in high school and I will be applying to universities this fall. My first choice is the University of California at Berkeley but we'll see what happens. I'm still not sure what I want to study. I'm thinking about world music but I'm not sure what I could do with that. I want to take more maths and science too. I'm hoping that over these next ten years I can connect all the aspects of my life: find what career I'm good at and one that helps me to serve the Faith more effectively, get married (after I finish travelling the world!) and then just take it from there.

Shamim Sadaghiyan I feel like I can do anything but it is very hard for me to make a decision. My immediate plans are to complete university after my service and maybe do some more service or teaching. My hopes for the next ten years are to complete my university studies, to learn to read and write Arabic and Farsi, to have a job wherever I go, to enjoy life and maybe to pioneer.

Leila Peters I want to live a long, happy life. My immediate plans are to finish high school, pray that I get a great scholarship, become something I like and help people.

My hopes for the next ten years are to finish high school and college, to get a degree in something that I like – something that really helps people and hopefully pays well – and perhaps to be married.

David McEwen I plan to study at 6th Form College (last two years at high school equivalent) next year. At the moment I want to enjoy the summer holidays and finish the rest of my exams successfully. I then hope to go to college, then maybe take a year of service. After that, I want to study at university.

Shirin Sadaghiyan It's so hard to look at the future, especially since I am still trying to live today. However, I have thought about my future countless times. All I can say is that I have no expectations except to be successful and happy in life and to be able to serve humanity and, to my utmost capacity, to help advance society. My immediate plans are more concrete because I have just graduated from the University of California, Irvine, with Bachelor degrees in English and Anthropology. I am one of the coordinators of our Bahá'í youth workshop and I will be working with them until I go on my year of service to Zambia at the end of August. I will be working at the Banani International Secondary School there. Ten years from now, I hope to have a PhD and be a university professor teaching my students about how they can make the world a better place (I don't know how yet) and I also hope to be married by then and have a family of my own.

9

Biographies of the Parents

Andrew Adams and his wife have been married for over 20 years. They have two adult children. Andrew and his wife are both teachers. They are lifelong Bahá'ís and have been determined to raise children who are spiritual, moral and happy. They live in the US.

Richard and Theresa Baker have two adult children. Richard is a retired structural engineer. Theresa's profession is secretarial with a vast number of interests in almost everything! They both became Bahá'ís several years before their children were born. They live in the UK.

Linda Bandari has two grown children and four grandchildren and plays an active role in their lives. For 20 years she managed a video post-production company that she and her husband owned until they sold it two years ago. She continues to work part-time for her husband's company, handling the company finances as she has for almost 30 years. Her hobbies include gardening, watercolour painting and cooking vegetarian dishes. The Bandaris live in the US.

Beth Bishop and her husband have three adult children. Beth is a social worker and has worked part-time in a fostering team since her youngest was five years old. Her husband, who is not a Bahá'í, is a lawyer. They have always lived in the same house in a village in England.

BIOGRAPHIES OF THE PARENTS

Angela Brown and her husband have six children and seven grandchildren. She has been a children's class and youth teacher in the Bahá'í community for 30 years and has been a pre-school, elementary, middle school and college teacher professionally. She is also the chairperson of the social science department at a university in the US. She has written a few Bahá'í children's books. Her husband is an English teacher and poet.

George and Mary Burke have four children – two girls and two boys, ranging in age from nine to university age. George is a video producer and Mary is a junior high school principal. They live in the US.

Tanya Charles and her husband have served as pioneers in the Pacific. They have three children ranging in age from seven to 14. Tanya was a stay-at-home mother and taught French privately during most of the years that their first two children were young but retired when the third was born. She has recently returned to work, teaching English as a second language to adults. Over the years Tanya has attended various parenting classes and has taught children's and junior youth classes. They live in the US.

Irene Dominguez and her husband have three daughters – two adults and one teenager. They live in Honduras.

Harriet Douglas is a 'wife, mother, homemaker, writer, cook, dishwasher – etc.!' She and her husband have three children - all 'lovely, loving, responsible adults and all married'. They live in the US.

Tom and Andrea Edwards have two children – one is in her twenties. The other passed away at the age of 19. Tom is self-employed as a consultant. Andrea is a special education teacher. They live in the US.

Margerie Gibson and her husband have a ten year old daughter, whom they home school. Margerie became a Bahá'í at the age of 17. She describes herself as 'a woman of many interests, talents and hobbies'. Her university degree was in horticulture, with emphasis in landscape design, but she received her diploma when she was three months pregnant with their daughter and chose be a fulltime mother at home with her. In the course of being a mother, she has discovered many interests, including wheel-thrown pottery, sewing, needlepoint, hiking and home schooling. She paints murals part time to bring in a little extra money. Her husband has been a Bahá'í for over 30 years and is currently a computer network administrator. The Gibsons live in the US.

Katayun Golshani and her husband have three adult children and one granddaughter. Her husband is a medical doctor. Katayun is a licensed marriage, family and child counsellor and family mediator in private practice. As well as many other things, she counsels families about the emotional needs of their children in times of separation and divorce and single parenting. She is a former producer, broadcaster and radio talk show host of a two-hour weekly live programme aimed at increasing the awareness of the public on psycho-social issues. She and her family travel nationally and internationally to serve the cause of global peace and prosperity. She has travelled extensively as a visiting professor and educational consultant to Europe, North and South America and, most recently, to China. The Golshanis live in the US.

John and Barbara Hartley have two adult sons. John owns a training and consulting business. He travels the world training managers and agents primarily for financial institutions. Barbara is an independent distributor for a health food supplement/beverage. They live in Canada.

Kevin Johnson and his wife, who died over 20 years ago, raised eight children – all of whom are now in their thirties and forties. Seven of his children are Bahá'ís, most of whom he considers to be active. The one child who is not a declared Bahá'í uses her prayer book extensively. Kevin has 12 grandchildren, all of whom are being raised as Bahá'ís. Kevin married his second wife in the 1990s. They live in the US.

Farzaneh Knight and her husband have two adult daughters, both of whom are ardent Bahá'ís, very close to their parents and have never caused them any grief at any age. The channels of communication have been wide open at all times. Farzaneh's husband is a legal interpreter/translator, Farzaneh is an educator. Both travel teach and lecture for the Faith. The Knights have served as pioneers in the Caribbean since 1988.

Edyth Lewis and her husband have three adult children and three grandchildren. Edyth is the managing director of a publishing company. Of their three children, two have served at the Bahá'í World Centre. For about ten years their middle child was not a Bahá'í but surprised them all by marrying a very active Bahá'í and has since become an active Bahá'í himself.

Lucy Matthews's great-grandmother was one of the early American Bahá'ís. Her mother, a late Hand of the Cause of God, met 'Abdu'l-Bahá when she was a child. She promptly became a Bahá'í. During her early adult years Lucy pioneered in South America and Latin America for several years. She later pioneered to western Europe. The Guardian told her to go either to Spain or to Portugal. She went to Portugal where she met her late husband. He later became a Bahá'í. They have one daughter. They didn't mean to have an only child but, after three miscarriages, they ended up with one. Lucy has one grandson. They live in the US.

Todd and Debbie McEwen met when they were Bahá'í youth at university and got married when they were 20. They have now been married for over 20 years and have three boys – ranging in age from 20 to 12. They have been involved in many Bahá'í events over the years and, in particular, they have worked with children's activities organized by Bahá'ís at a local and national level. Debbie is a teacher of dyslexic pupils and Todd is a management consultant. They live in the UK.

Bernice McKenzie and her husband are the parents of two daughters – one who passed away at the age of 31. The eldest is now a mother and is in her thirties. Bernice has been a secretary for 40 years. They all pioneered from North America to Australasia over 30 years ago where they were able to serve the Faith wholeheartedly. She says that 'the important thing to remember is that as our children were growing, my husband and I were growing as Baháʼís as well'.

Paul Oliver is divorced and now remarried. He has two adult children from his first marriage. Paul is a financial planner with his own business in the US. He has been a Baháʼí for over 30 years and has since served as a home front pioneer, youth workshop coordinator, author and speaker.

Linda Paulson has three adult children. A legal assistant. Linda has been a Baháʼí for over 30 years. In that time, she has pioneered and been travel teaching internationally. She and her family live and serve as home front pioneers in the American South. Living in the southern United States has not been easy for a Baháʼí family. She writes that her children were 'openly harassed, berated and threatened at school because they were Baháʼís. However, being friendly and warm, they made friends who invited them to church and they received a deeper understanding of Baháʼu'lláh's teachings through these experiences.'

Fatemeh Pfingston has two adult daughters. She has a Master's degree in clinical social work. She supervises a county contract agency in the US.

Donald Pope and his wife have two sons and three grandchildren. He holds a PhD in clinical/paediatric psychology and is executive director of an international educational foundation in Canada. He

BIOGRAPHIES OF THE PARENTS

is co-author of a popular parenting book. He and his wife travel and speak on moral development.

Marva Ross and her late husband have two sons, seven grandchildren and one great-grandson. Marva has a Master's degree in social work and worked as a family case worker and a medical social worker for a number of years. She has given courses on marriage and family life at various Bahá'í summer schools and is the author of a Bahá'í parenting book. She and her husband lived for many years in Haifa, Israel, where he served as a member of a Bahá'í institution. She lives in the US.

Nina Sadaghiyan was born in Iran. She and her husband live in the US and have two adult children.

Simon Scott and his wife became Bahá'ís in 1971 while attending university and were married in 1972. She is a maths teacher and, according to his accountants, Simon is called an 'investor', although what he actually does is trade energy futures for himself. They have two teenage daughters. They live in the US.

Michelle Sharpe and her husband live in the Caribbean. They have two children in their teens. Michelle works with a publication company. Her husband has a small food manufacturing company, manufacturing a range of hot pepper sauces, among other products. He is also a chef.

Grace Simpson lives in the US. She is an artist and a waitress. She is a single parent of an adult daughter.

Donna Smith and her husband have three sons and four grandchildren. They live in Canada. Her husband is a chartered accountant and has his own business. Donna helps out as well as serving as editor of a local monthly newspaper.

Celia Stewart and her husband have four adult children – three daughters and one son. Celia is the branch manager of a small library. Her husband works for the department of environmental quality for their state. They live in the US.

Melissa Taheri and her husband are both fourth-generation Baha'ís. They have two adult sons. Melissa has always worked part-time as a community health nurse. They live in the US.

Joe and Wilma Thompson have two adult daughters, Helen and Jennifer, who were both born deaf. They have one granddaughter. Joe is a medical doctor and Wilma is a dental hygienist. They live in the US.

Phoebe Untekar has been a Bahá'í for over 30 years. She is an import–export manager. She and her husband have three adult children, who are all actively involved in Bahá'í community life, and three grandchildren. They live in the US.

Julie Young and her husband have three adult children – two girls and one boy. Julie is a speech and language specialist. The Youngs live in the US.

Bibliography

'Abdu'l-Bahá. *Paris Talks*. London: Bahá'í Publishing Trust, 1967.

— *Selections from the Writings of 'Abdu'l-Bahá*. Haifa: Bahá'í World Centre, 1978.

Bahá'u'lláh. *Gleanings from the Writings of Bahá'u'lláh*. Wilmette, IL: Bahá'í Publishing Trust, 1983.

— *The Hidden Words*. Wilmette, IL: Bahá'í Publishing Trust, 1990.

— *The Kitáb-i-Aqdas*. Haifa: Bahá'í World Centre, 1992.

— *The Seven Valleys and the Four Valleys*. Wilmette, IL: Bahá'í Publishing Trust, 1991.

— *Tablets of Bahá'u'lláh revealed after the Kitáb-i-Aqdas*. Haifa: Bahá'í World Centre, 1978.

The Compilation of Compilations. Prepared by the Universal House of Justice 1963–1990. 2 vols. [Mona Vale NSW]: Bahá'í Publications Australia, 1991.

Directives from the Guardian. Compiled by Gertrude Garrida. New Delhi: Bahá'í Publishing Trust, 1973.

Lights of Guidance: A Bahá'í Reference File. Compiled by Helen Hornby. New Delhi: Bahá'í Publishing Trust, 2nd edn. 1988.

Nabíl-i-A'zam. *The Dawn-Breakers: Nabíl's Narrative of the Early Days of the Bahá'í Revelation*. Wilmette, IL: Bahá'í Publishing Trust, 1970.

Shoghi Effendi. *The Advent of Divine Justice*. Wilmette, IL: Bahá'í Publishing Trust, 1990.

— *Dawn of a New Day: Messages to India 1923–1957*. New Delhi: Bahá'í Publishing Trust, 1970.

The Universal House of Justice. *Messages from the Universal House of Justice 1963–1986: The Third Epoch of the Formative Age*. Wilmette, IL: Bahá'í Publishing Trust, 1996.

References

Chapter 1
1. Bahá'u'lláh, *Seven Valleys*, p. 2.
2. From a letter written on behalf of Shoghi Effendi, 22 November 1935, in *Dawn of a New Day*, pp. 56–7.
3. From a letter written on behalf of the Universal House of Justice, 22 November 1984, in *Compilation*, vol. 1, no. 981, p. 448.
4. From a letter written on behalf of the Universal House of Justice, 14 October 1982, in ibid. no. 979, p. 447.
5. 'Abdu'l-Bahá, *Selections*, pp. 80–1.
6. Bahá'u'lláh, *Gleanings*, p. 95.
7. Bahá'u'lláh, *Hidden Words*, Persian no. 5.
8. From a letter written on behalf of Shoghi Effendi, 16 March 1949, in *Compilation*, vol. 2, no. 1321, pp. 19–20.
9. Shoghi Effendi, *Directives of the Guardian*, p. 38.
10. From a letter written on behalf of Shoghi Effendi, 26 January 1935, in *Compilation*, vol. 1, no. 667, pp. 300–1.

Chapter 2
1. From a letter written on behalf of Shoghi Effendi, 9 July 1939, in *Compilation*, vol. 1, no. 673, p. 303.
2. 'Abdu'l-Bahá, *Selections*, p. 125.
3. From a letter written on behalf of the Universal House of Justice, 12 August 1975, in *Lights of Guidance*, no. 509, p. 152.
4. 'Abdu'l-Bahá, *Selections*, p. 135.
5. From a letter written on behalf of Shoghi Effendi, 22 July 1943, in *Compilation*, vol. 1, no. 682, p. 306.

REFERENCES

Chapter 3
1. 'Abdu'l-Bahá, *Bahá'í World Faith*, p. 384.
2. 'Abdu'l-Bahá, *Selections*, p. 136.
3. Bahá'u'lláh, *Hidden Words*, Arabic no. 22.

Chapter 4
1. From a letter written on behalf of Shoghi Effendi, 19 September 1946, in *Compilation*, vol.1, no. 816, p. 383.
2. 'Abdu'l-Bahá, in ibid. no. 185, p. 98.
3. From a letter written on behalf of Shoghi Effendi, 19 September 1946, in *Compilation*, vol.1, no. 816, p. 383.
4. From a letter of the Universal House of Justice, 10 February 1980, in the Universal House of Justice, *Messages 1963–1986*, para. 246.4, p. 435.
5. Shoghi Effendi, *Advent of Divine Justice*, p. 30.
6. From a letter of the Universal House of Justice, 13 July 1972, in *Lights of Guidance*, no. 1795, p. 528.
7. Shoghi Effendi, *Advent of Divine Justice*, p. 30.
8. Bahá'u'lláh, *Kitáb-i-Aqdas*, para. 159.
9. Bahá'u'lláh, *Tablets*, p. 23.
10. ibid.
11. See Shoghi Effendi, *Advent of Divine Justice*, p. 30.
12. Bahá'u'lláh, *Kitáb-i-Aqdas*, para. 159.
13. From a letter written on behalf of Shoghi Effendi, 4 November 1926, in *Compilation*, vol. 2, no. 1792, pp. 247–8.
14. From a letter of the Universal House of Justice, 9 November 1963, in *Lights of Guidance*, no. 1184, p. 353.
15. 'Abdu'l-Bahá, *Paris Talks*, p. 157.

Chapter 5
1. Bahá'u'lláh, *Hidden Words*, Persian no. 56.
2. From a letter written on behalf of Shoghi Effendi, 11 May 1945, in *Compilation*, vol. 1, no. 683, p. 306.
3. Nabíl-i-A'ẓam, *Dawn-Breakers*, p. 616.
4. Bahá'u'lláh, *Hidden Words*, Arabic no. 22.

Chapter 6
1. From a letter written on behalf of the Universal House of Justice, 18 December 1980, *Compilation*, vol. 1, no. 916, p. 414.
2. 'Abdu'l-Bahá, *Selections*, p. 118.
3. From a letter of the Universal House of Justice, 29 August 1965, in *Lights of Guidance*, no. 1236, p. 369.
4. From a letter of the Universal House of Justice, 1 February 1968, in ibid. no. 1237, pp. 369–70.

Chapter 7
1. 'Abdu'l-Bahá, in *Compilation*, vol. 1, no. 641, p. 290.
2. From a letter written on behalf of the Universal House of Justice, 9 August 1984, in ibid. vol. 2, no. 2165, p. 386.
3. From a letter written on behalf of Shoghi Effendi, 13 November 1940 in ibid. vol. 1, no. 676, p. 304.
4. From a letter written on behalf of Shoghi Effendi, 18 October 1932, in *Lights of Guidance*, no. 714, p. 212.
5. From a letter written on behalf of Shoghi Effendi, 11 January 1942, in *Compilation*, vol. 1, no. 679, p. 305.